Find Your Power

Boost Your Inner Strengths,
Break Through Blocks
and Achieve Inspired Action

Dr Chris Johnstone

NICHOLAS BREA   Y
PUBLISHIN(

LONDON • BOSTO

First published by
Nicholas Brealey Publishing in 2006
Reprinted 2007

3–5 Spafield Street	20 Park Plaza, Suite 1115A
Clerkenwell, London	Boston
EC1R 4QB, UK	MA 02116, USA
Tel: +44 (0)20 7239 0360	Tel: (888) BREALEY
Fax: +44 (0)20 7239 0370	Fax: (617) 523 3708

www.nicholasbrealey.com
www.chrisjohnstone.info

© Chris Johnstone 2006
The right of Chris Johnstone to be identified as the
author of this work has been asserted in accordance with
the Copyright, Designs and Patents Act 1988.

ISBN-10 1-85788-359-4
ISBN-13 978-1-85788-359-6

British Library Cataloguing in Publication Data
A catalogue record for this book is available from the
British Library.

All rights reserved. No part of this publication may be
reproduced, stored in a retrieval system, or transmitted,
in any form or by any means, electronic, mechanical,
photocopying, recording and/or otherwise without the
prior written permission of the publishers. This book
may not be lent, resold, hired out or otherwise disposed
of by way of trade in any form, binding or cover other
than that in which it is published, without the prior
consent of the publishers.

Printed in Finland by WS Bookwell on
Forest Stewardship Council certified paper.

Contents

Acknowledgements

The first few times I tried to write this book, I failed. Perhaps I wasn't ready then. But part of getting ready was finding allies to help me on my path; I'm grateful to everyone who has played a role in this. Alex Wildwood acted as a writing coach/supervisor. I met with him regularly over the three years it took me to produce the first draft. As I find it easier to talk than write, being interviewed by Mel McCree, Ly Vaillancourt and other friends helped me get my thoughts into words. Roz Chissick went through my second draft with a fine comb and helped me craft it more skilfully, while Julia McCutchen expertly guided me through the process of finding a publisher. Dave Baines produced the excellent cartoons that appear throughout the book.

My publisher Nicholas Brealey challenged me to transform my original proposal into a more reader-friendly book, and also offered essential guidance on how to do this. My editor Sally Lansdell did her magic with my manuscript and turned it into this book. Thanks also to the rest of the team at Nicholas Brealey Publishing.

I carried out nearly 100 interviews and over 30 people gave feedback on my finished manuscript. I'm sorry I'm not naming you all here, but you know I thank you. I'm also grateful to all the clients and course participants

I've learnt from, especially those who've given their permission for me to use their stories.

Lastly I wish to thank all my teachers, mentors and guides, particularly those I've quoted from in this book.

Introduction

Power is often thought of in terms of domination and control. This book takes a different approach. It describes how you find *personal* power, which I define as the ability to move in the direction you want to go. I use the term personal because the focus is on what *you* can do, rather than on what you can get others to do. This type of power strengthens your ability to face any situation and respond in a way that helps create the outcomes you desire.

Find Your Power invites you on a journey of developing inner strengths such as courage, determination, confidence, enthusiasm, clarity of purpose and the ability to deal with problems. Strengths like these are sometimes viewed as inherent qualities that some people have and others don't. We'll be looking at how they are also based on learnable strategies, so that whatever your current starting point, you can find ways of increasing and enhancing these valuable inner resources.

Why might you be interested in personal power? What benefits could it bring you? I regard power not as an end in itself, but as something that helps you achieve other things important to you. There may be concerns you want to address or directions you want to move in. When you think of the things you'd like to happen, whether in your personal life, your relationships, your work or our world, you give yourself reasons for being interested in power. This is the starting point. However, initial enthusiasm often hits two major stumbling blocks.

The first is having mixed feelings. Part of you is interested, but another part may be wary or even resistant. Power is a difficult word. It has negative associations that include corruption and ruthlessness. The problem here is not power itself, but the way it is so often viewed and expressed.

If you think of power as getting others to do things they don't want to do, you may associate it with bullying and manipulation. But the type of power this book promotes is designed to support your values rather than clash with them. The focus is on how you increase your ability to move in directions important to you, while also respecting the right of other people to make their own decisions.

A question we'll be exploring is what personal power is based on. If you think power depends on something you don't have, you're more likely to feel powerless. So if you want to do something, but don't have enough money, status, brains, good looks or whatever else you think is needed, it is easy to believe that the goal is beyond your power. This is the second block. How can we turn this one around?

Whatever the direction you want to head in, at least some of the obstacles you face are likely to lie within you. Doubt, fear, cynicism, apathy, disbelief and lack of confidence can all add to the barriers in your way. The approach I introduce helps you find ways through these. By strengthening your ability to deal with the inner obstacles, you put yourself in a better position to tackle any type of issue in your life. Here are some examples of the sort of things this can help with.

Some areas this book may help with
Increasing happiness, giving up smoking, taking up a musical instrument, starting your own business, losing weight, tackling global warming, improving working conditions, writing a book, enhancing relationships, finding a partner, recovering from depression, sorting out your finances, becoming more creative, surviving through times of crisis, increasing effectiveness at work, reducing stress, coping with illness, acting for world peace, creating more joy, clarifying purpose, moving on from your past if you want to, facing fears, becoming more determined, getting fitter, learning to laugh more, increasing self-confidence, developing a richly satisfying life.

The journey of finding your power

Whether you want to change your waistline or the world, your workplace or your state of mind, the process of altering anything requires a similar set of strengths. You need the *self-awareness* to know what you want, the *planning ability* to identify achievable next steps and the *motivation* to move into action. Any process of change is a journey and these strengths help get you started. The first part of this book, **The Power to Begin**, shows how to develop them. We will be looking at ways of getting clearer about what you *really* want and strategies for boosting your confidence to take those first important steps.

Once you start moving in the direction you want to go, it won't be long before you bump into some kind of obstacle. This isn't negative thinking. Obstacles offer an opportunity to develop new strengths and abilities; difficulties force you to think again, giving you an appetite for new skills and the deepening of wisdom. The second part of this book, **The Power to Move Through Blocks**, offers a toolkit to help you understand and work through many of the common resistances that block your path. We look at ways of dealing with fear, how to change stuck patterns of behaviour, creative problem-solving strategies and methods for transforming crisis and failure into turning points.

When you have found your way through the obstacles, you face a new set of challenges: how do you stop yourself from losing interest or getting disillusioned? The third part of the book, **The Power to Keep Yourself Going**, explores ways of maintaining the energy, enthusiasm and determination needed for any long-term project. I describe how to develop a context that supports the changes you want to make and also one that supports you in making them.

One of the main deepeners of determination is having a strong sense of purpose behind what you do. We will look at how inspiring purposes often come from seeing yourself as part of a bigger story. Personal power deepens when you act for something larger than your individual self. This could be your family, community, beliefs, country or world. But when you look at bigger-picture issues like organizations in crisis or the state of our planet, it is also easy to feel powerless. This is where we need the new ways of looking at power that this book introduces.

What this book is based on

I went to my first personal power workshop over 20 years ago. I saw how applying a simple collection of principles could help people turn their lives around. My life since then has been a quest of learning, studying and exploring this field. Over the last 15 years I've been running courses that pass on the insights and strategies I've found most useful. It is these I present in this book. I draw from a wide range of sources, but four in particular stand out as worth special mention.

The first is my work as a medical doctor and addictions specialist. Addictions can be thought of as a concentrated form of resistance to change, where someone can become so stuck in a pattern of behaviour that they continue doing it even when they know it is killing them. Yet many of my clients do find their way into recovery and my work with them has immensely deepened my understanding of what helps people change. By drawing on recent advances in the addictions treatment field, I outline approaches to strengthening motivation that are refreshingly effective. The usefulness of these extends far beyond just tackling addictions. As you will see, they can be applied to many areas of change.

The second source I draw from is the relatively new approach of positive psychology, which puts scientific method behind the study of happiness and the cultivation of strengths. Martin Seligman, a leading proponent, also developed one of the main psychological theories of depression,[1] known as the learned helplessness model. In this, he described how the experience of powerlessness was a factor in causing depression. His more recent research[2] has shown how we can develop learned *optimism*. As well as reducing our risk of depression, this can help us develop the resilience needed to bounce back from difficult situations. I draw on his findings and those of others within the positive psychology field.

Increasing motivation and optimism might seem irrelevant if what you want to change is beyond your power to influence. Yet many of the assumptions that commonly limit power are based on an eighteenth-century approach. My third source is the modern holistic approach to science that lies behind chaos theory and systems thinking. This can lead to breakthroughs in the way we view power and influence. I will show how ideas like the butterfly effect offer the essential upgrade in thinking needed to bring personal power into the twenty-first century.

As part of my research for writing this book, I carried out in-depth interviews with a wide range of people. I asked them how they found their power and also what blocked it. The fourth source, therefore, is the human experience of the people I interviewed. Their stories provide real-life examples that demonstrate the tools and insights I describe. I also include my own experience, as this is what has most convinced me that thinking about power in new ways really makes a difference.

Thinking differently about power

In the late 1980s I worked as a doctor in a London hospital. My contract was for an average of 88 hours a week, although with compulsory overtime there were often weeks when I'd put in well over 100 hours. Not surprisingly, I became completely exhausted. Thinking this was a crazy way to work, I started asking my colleagues what we could do to improve our conditions. 'We don't have the power here,' I was told, 'nothing we can do will make any difference.'

In the phrase 'we don't have the power here', power is a noun. Whenever you think of power as a thing that others have and you don't, you effectively pull the plug on your own authority. This leads to what I call the 'inner power cut', where it seems that nothing you can do will make any difference. But you can also think of power as a verb (for example 'I power myself'). Verbs refer to things that you *do* rather than *have*. So whenever you're in a situation where you're feeling underpowered, this way of thinking focuses attention on what you can do to respond.

Whatever the situation, you always have choices about your response. Some choices move you in the direction you want to go, while others take you further away. When you explore your options and choose one that moves you, even if only a small amount, in the direction you want to go, you start a ball rolling. I think of this as the journey approach to change. With this way of thinking, you don't have to have a clearly mapped-out blueprint for success before you can begin. You just focus on steps you can take from where you are, wherever that is.

So how did this approach help me when I was working all those crazy hours as a hospital doctor?

My story

In the 1980s, not many people knew about the hours problem. Most doctors were unwilling to speak out for fear that this would damage their careers. So the problem remained hidden and slowly got worse. I knew surgeons who performed operations after working round the clock for over 50 hours without any sleep. Mistakes were made through sheer exhaustion and as many as one in four junior doctors[3] (or residents as they're called in the US) showed evidence of clinical depression. I was so appalled that I joined the small group of doctors who were campaigning on this issue. I became a whistle-blower and started to talk to the press about what was going on.

I agreed to speak with a television news team, but the evening before the interview was due to take place a hospital manager phoned me at home. He told me that if I went ahead with the broadcast, I would need to watch out for my future. Nevertheless, there are times when a situation cries out for people to come forward – so I did.

In spite of the growing media interest, there was no change in my working conditions. At the time my job was in a busy obstetrics unit where I could work over 50 hours in a single shift. The grinding sleep deprivation led me to become seriously depressed. I even began to think about suicide. A colleague who was concerned about me suggested taking legal action against my employers. I consulted a lawyer, but he told me the case was a no-hoper and might even be laughed out of court. A second opinion said something similar. Then a lawyer friend told me she saw things differently. She was so horrified by the conditions I was working under that she agreed to take on the case for free. With her help, I issued a writ challenging the legal basis of my contract.

Taking my employers to court created massive publicity. My picture was on the front page of newspapers and friends the other side of the world saw me on their television news. Now the issue of junior doctors' hours was placed firmly in the public eye. At that time I had no funding and couldn't afford to pursue the case on my own, but a newspaper article mentioned this and people started sending me money. In the first few months I received over 200 letters of support and thousands of pounds in donations. A leading barrister provided his services free of charge and a team of people stepped forward to offer their support. There had been widespread concern about the dangers of such working hours and people felt pleased to be able to contribute towards a positive step for change.

Six years and ten court hearings later, I finally won my case. Junior doctors still work long hours compared with most other groups, but their conditions have improved dramatically. The campaign was a success.

Turning things around

Many people asked me how I found the determination to stick with this case when there were so many obstacles in its way. At first my situation was bleak and there didn't seem much chance of improvement. But one thing that gave me inspiration was the idea that our lives are a bit like adventure stories. These often begin from a similar place of gloom. The little hobbit Frodo didn't seem to stand much of a chance at the beginning of *The Lord of the Rings*, but that didn't put him off. Stories similar to this have been told for thousands of years, not just for their entertainment value, but also because they teach important principles of personal power. I'd like to identify a few features of such stories that can help us find our power. The first of these I call the *turning*.

How many adventure stories can you think of that start with a gloomy beginning yet still manage to find their way to a happy ending? The plot in these tales usually revolves around the sequence of events that allows a reversal of fortunes, or turning, to occur. The message transmitted is that no matter how dreadful things are at the start, positive changes, even if they initially seem unlikely, are possible. This turning doesn't happen by itself though; it is dependent on active steps taken by the main characters in the story.

This perspective offered an alternative to the widespread pessimism I encountered in my colleagues. It reminded me that life is mysterious and can sometimes surprise us. It also reminded me that if I wanted a turning to occur, then I needed to become part of the story that helped this to happen.

Another feature of adventure tales is the way the central characters become transformed over the course of the story. Often they start out seeming puny and inept, only to reveal unsuspected strengths at crucial moments. There is an important lesson here. If we judge our abilities by how we are when we're at the beginning of something, we fail to take into account the way that facing later challenges can help us grow into more capable versions of ourselves. Like muscles that develop through lifting weights, inner strengths are found by engaging with situations where they're needed. And when we take steps in the directions most important to us, the journey itself acts as training that helps us grow in our abilities.

The good news is that we don't have to do all of this on our own. There will always be sources of help if we can see them, and a necessary part of any adventure is the seeking out of allies. In stories, the role of the ally is to help the hero or heroine grow in power so that they are not blocked by the obstacles in their way. They support by passing on essential information, offering encouragement, providing training and supplying vital tools.

This book aims to serve a similar function. It is designed to be one of your allies: to help you grow in personal power so that you can more easily move towards the goals that are important to you, facing and dealing with the challenges on the way.

Finding power in the way you read this book

We think of a book as powerful when it has impact on our lives, inspiring us to breakthroughs and new ways of seeing things. There is certainly much in the chapters ahead that can do that. But how much of the power is in the book and how much is in the way you read it? Is it possible to read in a powerful manner, so that you gain more from a piece of writing? Here are three suggestions for how you might do that with this book.

1 **Try it out**: each chapter has 'Try this' boxes like the one below. They invite you to test out personal power tools and principles in your life. Obviously it is your choice whether you do this, but the more you use this book rather than merely reading it, the greater the benefit you'll gain.

2 **Memory pegs**: have you read a great book but struggled six months later to remember what it said? A memory peg is anything that helps you retain the information you want to hang on to. Here is an example.

> ### *Try this: Memory pegs*
> *After reading each chapter, ask yourself two questions:*
> ◆ *Is there anything in this chapter I can start using now?*
>   *If you've used something as well as read about it, it is easier to remember.*
> ◆ *What bits do I still want to remember in six months' time?*
>   *Find some way of recording the key points you don't want to forget. Keeping a personal power notebook is a good way of doing this.*

3 **Have good reasons**: while I encourage you to try the exercises and memory peg each chapter, powerful reading involves taking whatever approach works best for you. If you prefer to dip in and out or skim read, then please do. However, it is useful to ask why it might be worth the effort of a more active approach. This question points you towards a central ingredient of personal power: having good reasons. If you have purposes you want this book to help you with, these provide you with reasons for reading at a deeper level. To begin, or continue, the journey of finding your power, you need motives. It might be that you're clear what these are for you. If you're not, the good news is that motivation, like other inner strengths, can be cultivated. The first chapter shows how to do this.

Part I

The Power to Begin

*"Tell me, what is it that you plan to do
with your one wild and precious life?"*
Mary Oliver

1

The Call to Adventure

The vital first step in finding your power can be summarized by the following words: hearing within yourself the call to adventure and choosing to answer it. We will look at what this means, how to do it and also how such inner calls to action can get blocked. The place to start, though, is with an insight into the nature of human energy.

How to energize yourself

In traditional Chinese medicine, the concept of *chi* doesn't just refer to energy, but to an energy that also has direction. The principle here is that personal energy and direction are linked. When you find a clear sense of purpose or direction, it energizes you.

This is true in storytelling too. A plot that has no direction is boring. But as soon as a purpose arises that calls the attention of the central character, then the energy of the story starts to rise. It has somewhere to go. See if you notice the points in the following paragraph at which the energy shifts.

I spent the last hours of the twentieth century in my home city of Bristol. The council had organized a huge street party, with bands playing in the city squares and a massive firework display. But somehow I felt a bit bored by the whole affair. I wandered through the crowds with my brother David, feeling aimless and lacking in energy. I wasn't in a party mood and I thought about getting an early night. Then in the distance, I heard someone drumming. A lone djembe player sat on a street corner. A thought danced through my mind: how would it be to go back home, get some drums and then join forces with the djembe man? 'Wow!' I thought. 'I love drumming, that is exactly how I'd most like to celebrate the start of a new millennium.' I was excited, and my brother liked the idea too. We raced home, picked up some percussion, and with a new energy we returned. We drummed till the small hours of a new century, a crowd around us dancing in the street. It was fantastic.

The mythologist Joseph Campbell[1] introduced the term 'call to adventure' to describe that moment early on in a story when the main character becomes aware of an attractive or compelling motive. They are called to do something, go somewhere or bring about some change. This is when the plot takes off. The same thing happens in our lives. When an attractive possibility calls to us, it pulls us out of the doldrums. When we choose to answer that call, we give ourselves purpose and direction in a way that can energize us.

That is what happened for me when I heard that djembe sound. Once I'd made the decision to go and join the drumming, I was amazed at how my physical energy lifted. Earlier I'd been feeling lethargic but, with a positive vision to head for, I walked so fast my brother found it difficult to keep up with me. I had energy in my feet because I had a reason for walking that was important to me. That reason acted as a key, opening up a power source within me.

Calls to adventure are usually triggered by an external event, where something happens that stimulates the desire or demand for a particular course of action. Here are some examples:

◆ *After a conversation with a friend, Susie realizes she wants to change her career.*
◆ *Being inspired by a great concert, Lizzie decides to take up a musical instrument.*
◆ *Reading a book about a prisoner who escapes, Simon considers how he might escape from a situation he feels trapped in.*

With the call we become alerted to the pull in a particular direction. What tugs at us might be the attractiveness of a new possibility or an existing motivation reinforced by recent events. By recognizing how such openings of interest are prompted, we can develop ways of stimulating our own enthusiasm. Rather than waiting for those occasional inspired moments, we can learn to trigger motivational boosts ourselves. First, though, it helps to have some understanding of the basis of human motivation.

Understanding motivation

In order to move towards any goal, two things are needed: having the will and finding the way. *Will* is about motivation and *way* is about ability. These two influence each other. For example, discovering a better way of doing something can boost your enthusiasm for doing it. But you're unlikely to look for a better way unless you have the will to do this. So how do you develop the will to begin finding the way?

The secret of motivation is having good reasons behind what you do. The more compelling your motives, the stronger your motivation is likely to be. You can boost your willpower simply by identifying the most convincing reasons you can think of for what you want to do. It is easier to feel the enthusiasm that comes from having your heart in what you do when you are clear why you are doing it. If you can't find good reasons, then you need to create some, or question whether you really want to continue what you're doing.

Motivation grinds to a halt when there are also convincing reasons for *not* doing something. Being stuck between competing agendas saps energy and makes it difficult to move forward. But this is something that can be worked with. One of the most successful treatments in the addictions field is a relatively new approach called motivational interviewing.[2] A one-hour session of this at the beginning of an existing treatment programme has been shown to lead to measurable improvements in outcome a year later.[3] Being clearer about motivation leads clients to make better use of the treatment programme they go through. And the way they became clearer is by looking at the different pulls within them, so that they can work out what is calling them most strongly.

At the core of motivational interviewing is the idea that you make your own argument for change. You're the best person to convince yourself because you know what you find most convincing. When you hear yourself express the argument that sways you, you talk yourself into the changes you want to make. Let's look at how you can apply this.

Motivational awareness

The first step to understanding your own motivation is to pay attention to its rises and falls, noticing the factors that influence it. I think of this as developing motivational awareness. What are the things that perk up your interest and enthusiasm? What makes you decide that something is worth doing? When you describe the motives that call you deeply, you remind yourself of what you need to follow in order to feel motivated.

> **Try this: A motivational awareness tool**
> At random intervals throughout each day, pause for a moment and ask yourself these three questions:
> ◆ What am I doing?
> ◆ Why am I doing this?
> ◆ Where is it taking me?
> I refer to these as the 'awareness questions'.[4]

If you can't find good reasons behind what you're doing, ask yourself what would happen if you stopped. If negative consequences would follow, you have a reason to continue. But when you stop doing things you don't have good enough reasons for, you clear a space. This makes room for something new. It can be a step in finding your power.

One night recently I was watching a film on television. I wasn't enjoying it much, but found myself glued to the chair as if hypnotized. I asked myself the awareness questions; it broke the spell. Sometimes I enjoy watching television, but this wasn't one of those times and so I didn't have a good reason to continue watching. I switched it off and got on with something I wanted to be doing instead.

Asking yourself what you really want

When you ask yourself what you *really* want you immediately bring into focus something that motivates you. The word 'really' encourages you to go beneath the surface and touch the areas that matter to you most. These deeper motivations may be different from what you might seem to want on the surface. One of the people I interviewed told me about a dream he had that illustrates this.

> **Dave's dream**
> Dave dreamt that he had died. He was called in to see God, who sat on a red leather armchair, smoking a cigar and sipping port.
>
> God invited Dave to sit down next to him and asked, 'How was that then?'
>
> Dave reflected on how his life had been and replied, 'Very nice, thank you.'
>
> Then he paused, frowned to himself and added, 'Only I didn't get to do what I really wanted to do.'
>
> God looked at Dave with a friendly, gentle smile and asked, 'Why was that then?'

At the time of the dream, Dave appeared to be very successful, earning good money and recently having been promoted in his job. Only he wasn't doing what he *really* wanted to do. Dave's passion was for art and the process of making things. But he was so busy with his job that he didn't have time for this. His dream was a wake-up call that told him his life was off course. The more he thought about this, the more motivated he became to make a change. Dave was experiencing his call to adventure.

When you follow the path that seems most important to you, you are acting from what psychologists call intrinsic motivation. This is the motivation that comes from the inside, rather than that based on external rewards. It tends to be a much more powerful source of motivation.

Awareness of your own mortality

Some years ago I found a lump in my scrotum and became worried that I might have cancer. When a scan showed the lump to be benign, I heaved a sigh of relief. But the thought that I might have had a life-threatening illness stopped me in my tracks and forced a re-examination of my life's direction. I wondered what I would do differently if I only had a year or two left to live. When something is in short supply we have good reasons to be careful about how we use it, particularly if what's running out is the rest of our life.

This may initially sound morbid, but awareness of our mortality can be a powerful trigger for change. There are many inspiring examples of people who've dramatically transformed their lives for the better following close brushes with death. Like Dave with his dream, they had a wake-up call and they responded to it.

Fortunately, you don't need to wait until you have a terminal diagnosis before this can happen for you. All it takes is a willingness to look at the chunk of life you've got left, however long that is, and to ask yourself what you would really like to happen. This question invites you to describe your vision of how you would like your life to be. When you have a positive vision to head for, this becomes your call to adventure. It gives you a reason for getting out of bed in the morning with enthusiasm rather than reluctance.

Reminding myself of my mortality encourages me to cut through to the things that matter most. If I only had a year to live, there are plenty of things that I wouldn't want to waste my time doing. So why do them now? There are also things that I really do want to do before I die. So why not start them now? When I take the steps that are important to me, I reduce the risk that one day I'll look back on my life with regret. It prompts me to head out for the things my heart is in most. It also gives me a very good reason to develop my personal power. But what do you do if you're not sure what you want?

Taking steps to become clearer

If you don't have a clear, positive vision to head for, the first question to ask yourself is whether you would like one. If you would, then this becomes your call, as the goal you're aiming for is greater clarity about what you want. Sometimes our life purpose is revealed to us a little at a time, so that what we see is just the next bit of it. It may only be much later, when we look back on our life as a whole, that the many parts fit together to create a clearer picture of what it has all been about. A saying I find helpful is: 'Rather than looking for the purpose of life, look for a life with purpose.' Each positive vision, even if it is only for the next few hours, gives your life at that moment a purpose and direction to head in.

If you're not sure what you want, another approach is to ask yourself whether there's anything you *don't* want.

For example, are there unwelcome possibilities or realities you would like to move away from? Vision and concern are both powerful motivators, one being a recognition of what attracts you, the other identifying what you want to distance yourself from. Some people are motivated more by the pull of *towards* reasons, others by the push of *away from* reasons. You can find out what motivates you most strongly by asking the awareness questions (see p 18) when you are doing something you feel particularly engaged in. When you ask where this is taking you, do you describe what you're moving towards or away from? By noticing what sort of motivational triggers most powerfully inspire you, you can build up a working knowledge of what strengthens your will.

When you make a decision that you want to become clearer about your purpose, you start a process of curiosity and discovery. You pay attention to your reactions, noticing when things register highly on your inner Richter scale of importance. You are following the trail of an inspiring purpose. One of the clues that you could be on the right track is when you find something you don't want to look at.

Inspirational dissatisfaction

Recently I had some trouble with a leaky tap. I found the incessant 'drip, drip, drip' of the water so annoying. Then I discovered that if I put a cloth under the tap, I couldn't hear it dripping. Peace of mind at last! The problem was that months later, I still had a leaky tap. Over time it had got significantly worse, although now it didn't bother me so much. Because I'd fixed my irritation rather than the tap, I hadn't found the motivation to get it repaired.

I think of this story when I'm feeling troubled because it reminds me how feelings of dissatisfaction can be useful wake-up calls. A common way for motivation to get blocked is when good reasons for change are ignored because they are uncomfortable to look at. I've often heard people say 'I don't want to think about that because it upsets me', yet upset, anger, disappointment and fear are all signals that can alert us to the need to tackle an issue. These can be powerful motivators: when we are bothered by something we are most likely to act to change it. Self-help authors Napoleon Hill and W Clement Stone describe this as 'inspirational dissatisfaction'.[5]

Another example of the same motivational principle at work is when addicts hit rock bottom. When my clients aren't bothered by the consequences of their drinking, they're unlikely to want to tackle the issue. But when something goes badly wrong and this shocks or disturbs them, it can become the wake-up call that motivates positive change.

If you are feeling dissatisfied with any aspect of your life right now, you are doing the right thing by reading this book. Think of this as the beginning of the story. The dissatisfaction is your call to adventure. It gives you a good reason to be interested in finding your power. What we'll be exploring is how to use both your dissatisfactions and your positive visions to motivate yourself. And a useful starting point is to look at how you can deepen the motivation you already feel. When you strengthen your will at the beginning of a process, it can help you maintain the resolve needed to find a way forward.

> **Try this: Inspirational dissatisfaction**
> On a blank piece of paper, complete the following
> sentences:
> ◆ The things that bother me most are...
> ◆ My biggest concerns for the future are...
> See if you can write a page for each sentence.

Over a decade ago, I carried out some research looking at workshops I was running to help people find their power to respond to global issues. Opinion polls[6] show that most people consider the condition of our world to be getting worse, and this is an area where they commonly feel powerless. Yet simple exercises like the one above, when carried out as a listening exercise in pairs, gave people an opportunity to express their concerns in a way that deepened their motivation. A year later, in a follow-up study,[7] over 90 per cent of respondents reported that the workshop had strengthened their feeling that they could make a difference in the world.

Finding the want behind the should

Feelings of concern play an important role in prompting us to look at and address challenging areas. But they may not be enough to help us sustain enthusiasm for what we do. For that we need to identify the positive things we're giving ourselves by taking steps in a particular direction. I think of this as finding the *want* behind the *should*. When I interviewed Tim, he told me how he'd been able to use this approach to give up smoking.

Tim had smoked for decades and had regarded this as one of his major pleasures in life. He particularly enjoyed sitting outside after an evening meal and watching the stars while having a cigarette. It was a time he felt at peace. Even though he coughed every morning and had concerns about his health, this hadn't been a strong enough reason to get him to quit. Then one day a friend got Tim thinking in a completely different way.

'Smoking is obviously important to you, Tim,' his friend said. 'I just wonder what would happen to your life if you didn't do it any more, so that all the time, money and attention that go into smoking were available for you to use in some other way.'

As Tim added up in his mind all that went into supporting his smoking habit, he could see that it was a big drain on his resources. There were things he really wanted to do in his life, and he began to recognize that smoking was holding him back. In the past he'd always thought of 'giving up' as something that he should do but that involved having a pleasurable activity taken away from him. Now he saw it differently: smoking was taking away the resources he needed to move towards his dreams. Tim was excited by the vision of what might be possible if he liberated himself from tobacco addiction, and this gave him the willpower he needed to stop.

Tim's story is a good example of how finding a better or more convincing reason can make the process of positive change easier. Tim was particularly motivated by 'moving towards' reasons, so his health concerns weren't nearly as compelling as his dreams for the future. Each time he felt tempted to smoke, he'd say to himself: 'I just wonder what will happen to my life if I don't.' Every craving refused was seen as a mini-victory in his adventure of moving towards the things he wanted most.

This illustrates how motivation is powerfully influenced by the way we look at a situation. When we see how an action contributes to our deepest hopes and motives, we uncover good reasons that can strengthen our will. But there is still a problem if what we most want to happen seems impossible.

What comes before how

When I started campaigning about junior doctors' hours, two things people said to me were 'you can dream all you like, it won't make any difference' and 'there's no point worrying about something you can't do anything about'. If something really is impossible to change, then having visions or concerns about it might seem a waste of time. But if there is a way of doing something and we just haven't found it yet, then dreams or worry might be the essential motivators that inspire the search for a breakthrough. The central question here, then, is: 'How do we know for sure whether something is impossible?'

Many breakthroughs are likely to seem unrealistic before they occur. That is why they are seen as breakthroughs, because they *break through* a previously accepted view of what was achievable. If you ever find yourself wondering whether to dismiss a dream as impossible, it is worth first remembering the words of Lord Kelvin, the distinguished scientist and President of the Royal Society, who in 1895 announced authoritatively:

Heavier-than-air flying machines are impossible.

When Thomas Edison invented the electric light bulb, he knew what he wanted to do but he didn't know how to do it. He tried thousands of different ways that all failed. He kept trying because his vision gave him a good reason to continue. It was an exciting idea that he believed in. Eventually he found a way to make it work. This example illustrates an important principle of creativity: *what* comes before *how*.

If we dismiss our vision of what we want because we can't immediately see how to do it, we stop ourselves ever finding a way. This is why I like the idea of seeing our lives as an adventure story. When we set out on such a quest, the goal might initially seem unrealistic, but that doesn't stop us. We recognize that things often seem impossible when we can't see how to do them, but if we begin the process of searching for a way we're more likely to find one.

What is your call?

If you've picked this book up and read this far, you've already heard a call that you've chosen to answer. You're on the journey of finding and deepening your personal power. But what is it that calls you? The next exercise can help make this clearer.

When you focus your attention on what you want to be doing and why you want to do this, you reinforce your interest and strengthen your will. This is the starting point. Now we need to develop the way. The next chapter provides an essential step towards this.

Try this: What is your call to adventure?
- *If this book could help you do one thing, what would it be?*
- *Why is that important to you?*
- *Repeat this process as many times as you like, each time asking: 'If there was one other thing, what would it be?'*

Power Points

1 Calls to adventure are motivational impulses: you feel an inner call to do something, go somewhere or bring about some change. Choosing to answer these calls gives your life purpose and direction in a way that can energize you. This is the starting point of finding your power.

2 Rather than waiting passively for those occasional inspired moments, you can learn to trigger motivational boosts yourself. Here are seven ways of doing this:

- **Motivational awareness**: when you name the motives that deeply call you, you remind yourself of what you need to follow in order to feel motivated.
- **Asking yourself what you really want**: the word *really* encourages you to go beneath the surface and touch areas that matter to you most.
- **Awareness of your own mortality**: if there's something you really want to do, reminding yourself you've limited time left can prompt you to get on and do it.

♦ **Take steps to become clearer**: if you're not sure what you want, the desire for a clearer purpose can become your call to adventure. It starts you on a journey of looking for something that inspires you.

♦ **Inspirational dissatisfaction**: motivation gets blocked when good reasons for change are ignored because they are uncomfortable to look at. Feelings of disturbance, alarm and dissatisfaction can activate your motivational energy.

♦ **Find the 'want' behind the 'should'**: finding and tapping into your deeper enthusiasms maintains motivation better than acting out of obligation.

♦ **Recognize that 'what' comes before 'how'**: if you dismiss an attractive idea because you can't immediately see how to achieve it, you stop yourself from finding a way. Knowing *what* you want is just the starting point. Then comes the journey of finding out *how*.

3 If this book could help you do one thing, what would it be? Why do you want that? Each time you ask these questions, you clarify your call to adventure.

2

A New Story of Power

*B*y the time the average child in the western world finishes their schooling, they are likely to have witnessed over 18,000 murders[1] and 100,000 acts of violence[2] on television. We learn by watching others, and the model of power transmitted by much modern media can be summarized by the following words: 'Do as I say or I'll bash you!'

If you value relationships, kindness or honesty, the idea that you need to be ruthless in order to be powerful can put you off. The way forward here is to develop a different way of thinking about power. In this chapter, we look at five shifts in perspective that make power both more attractive and more easily within our reach. These shifts are:

◆ *from control to influence*
◆ *from physics to psychology*
◆ *from big to small*
◆ *from noun to verb*
◆ *from 'they should' to 'I will'.*

From control to influence

When I ask people to complete the sentence 'By power I mean...', the first word that often pops out is 'control'. Yet viewing power in terms of control can place a psychological obstacle in the way of feeling powerful.

Here's an example. I walk into a crowded room and ask: 'Who's in control here?' People look at each other and then point me towards a door at the back. Behind that door sits the one in charge. When we think of power in terms of control, this person has it and the others don't. But if I walk into the same crowded room and ask instead 'Who has influence here?' everyone present might think they have some. A simple shift in perspective can turn power on.

A friend of mine was recently in conflict with her boss. Describing the situation, she said: 'He's the one in control here, there's nothing I can do.' Because control tends to be thought of in all-or-nothing terms, one side is seen to have it all, while the other side may feel they have nothing. My friend located all the power in her boss, and she was left feeling powerless.

When we looked at the situation together, it was clear that there were many ways she could influence how this conflict developed. Through the choices she made about how to respond, she could alter the direction in which things went. This is different from controlling what happens. Each choice is like a vote that can steer the outcome a particular way. Things may still not always work out quite how we want them to, but using our votes of influence like this does make a difference to what happens.

One choice available to my friend was to hang on to her resentment and continue feeling hostile. This would have effects on her body language and tone of voice, making her appear distant and unfriendly. Her boss might see this as her being uncooperative and stroppy, leading to rebound effects on his behaviour. As irritation and resentment get bounced between these two people, a vicious cycle is created (see Figure 2.1) that maintains and amplifies their relationship difficulty.

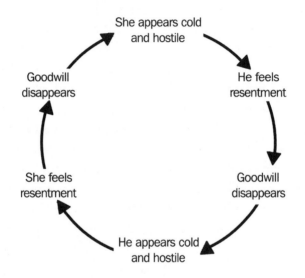

Figure 2.1 A vicious cycle that maintains and amplifies conflict

My friend recognized what had been happening and didn't like it. She wanted an alternative to feeling like a victim and the tension of resentment that went with this. Together we mapped out the issues involved in the conflict and she then arranged a meeting with her boss to discuss these. The conflict helped create an opportunity to address concerns that had been grumbling in the background for ages. Tackling these issues led to an improvement in my friend's relationship with her employer. She found her power by recognizing her role in the conflict and seeing how she could change it.

This story provides examples of at least four different types of power. The first is *power over*, which is the more traditional view, where one person has a dominant position over someone else. People have this sort of power when they can get others to do things they don't want to do. It is linked to being in charge or control. But my friend found a different type of power when she looked at the issues involved and summoned up the courage to approach her boss. Because it is based on inner strengths like confidence and determination, we can think of this approach as *power from within*.

Yet another type of power emerged when my friend and her boss were able to act together to address the conflict issues between them. This is the power of cooperative relationships, referred to as *power with*. It involves people acting with one another towards common goals.

The fourth type of power is more subtle. To recognize it, you need to take a step back and consider how individual actions contribute to a bigger picture and a larger process of change. For example, organizations and cultures evolve over time as a result of many smaller steps taken by individuals. By openly discussing her concerns with her boss, my friend played a part in developing a more democratic working culture in her organization. As bigger changes like this happen through the cumulative effect of smaller changes, this type of power is referred to as *power through*.

Power through can also be seen on an individual level, where significant personal shifts occur over time through many smaller increments. Each action, by itself, might be seen as insignificant. It is only when you step back and see how they all fit together that you recognize their power. For example, the conversation I had with my friend contributed to the larger process of her finding her power within her workplace. It was one step on a larger journey. There were also other things she did that helped her find her power, such as exercising regularly, going on personal development workshops and eating healthily. As each of our smaller decisions has an influence, power acts through them.

If you ever find yourself facing a situation that appears to be beyond your control, these different ways of viewing power open up new possibilities for moving forward. Rather than thinking 'it is out of my control, there is nothing I can do', the shift in focus from control to influence leads to a different understanding of what power is based on.

♦ *Power from within* is based on finding and using strengths within yourself like courage, resourcefulness and determination.
♦ *Power with* is based on finding common purpose with others and developing good relationships.
♦ *Power through* is based on recognizing how larger processes of change can act through you and the many small steps you take.

Each of these three dimensions of personal power can be used to turn around feelings of powerlessness.

An advantage of aiming for influence rather than control is that it makes it possible to be powerful without there having to be a power struggle. Battles for control tend to involve one person or group taking it away from others. But when people let go of the need to dominate or control others, this allows room for vastly improved relationships. Both sides influence each other, and when one person finds the courage to speak or live their truth, this can inspire others to do so too. With this model of power, one person's gain doesn't have to be at someone else's expense. However, this does depend on the methods used to gain influence. This is where the next shift in thinking is important.

From physics to psychology

From the perspective of classical physics, power is defined by an equation that has force as one of its main ingredients:

$$\text{Power} = \frac{\text{force x distance}}{\text{time}}$$

This way of thinking has spread far beyond physics. For example, in the equation above, the more force you have the greater the power. This assumption can be seen at work in many feature films and television dramas, as well as in international politics. What it leads to is a tendency to use force and threat as ways of expressing power, particularly when there is a conflict. This approach may make engaging television, but it often destroys personal and working relationships. If we're to move away from violence and bullying, we need a different way of thinking about power.

If we think of obstacles in our way as similar to doors that are locked to us, the view of power based on physics considers how much force is needed to gain entry. Another approach is simply to ring the doorbell. When you do, what's transmitted is not force but information.

If the person on the other side has heard the call and wants to open the door to you, no forced entry is necessary. And what would make them want to open the door? As soon as you start considering things like awareness (doorbell ringing) and motivation (do they want to answer?), you move from a *physical* view of power to a *psychological* one.

This shift is from a view of power dependent on force to one based on information. When facing an obstacle, the question changes from 'How much force can I bring to bear?' to 'What do I need to learn in order to change this?' In dealing with conflicts between people, this approach leads to exploration of issues and understanding of perspectives. Listening is needed here, rather than force of weapons or argument. From an informed position it becomes possible to design win–win outcomes where both sides benefit. This is what happened when my friend opened up a dialogue with her employer. Addressing the issues led to an improved relationship from which both sides benefited.

While the old 'power over' model acknowledges the strategic value of information where this gives competitive advantage, the personal power approach takes a much broader view. The purpose of this book, for example, is to transmit the sort of information that can help you open the door to more power in your life. There are also some types of knowledge that you can't find in books, such as inner knowledge, knowing what you really want and also what you don't want.

Personal blocks are often related to some part of us not wanting to open the door to a particular change. When you're feeling resistant to doing something, working through mixed feelings and clarifying the positive reasons for change is a more effective start-up strategy than bullying or forcing yourself. Tim, in the last chapter, had tried forcing himself to give up smoking. It didn't work. But when he found the right motivational button to press, he experienced the call to adventure that inspired him to change. This is finding the power of will.

Central to the psychological approach to power is an understanding that the way we think and feel about a goal will influence our ability to reach it. It is important to address the issue of how we look at power, because having mixed feelings here can create resistance to the process of becoming powerful. The following 'Try this' can help identify whether this might be an issue for you.

> **Try this: Complete the following sentences**
> ◆ *People who are powerful tend to be... (identify at least five features).*
> ◆ *If I were to imagine power as an article of clothing it would be...*

When I use this exercise in my workshops, people usually identify both attractive and not so attractive features of being powerful. As well as 'able to get things done' and 'clear thinking', responses have also included 'blamed when things go wrong' and 'dishonest'. When I've asked people to imagine power as an article of clothing, responses have included suits of armour, jackets with hidden weapons and those huge protective shoulder pads worn by American footballers.

How do you view power? If you picture it as something that is uncomfortable to wear, then you have a good reason to avoid being powerful. An important step in finding your power is developing a way of thinking about it that is attractive to you and that doesn't clash with your values. This is where your story of power is important.

I use the term 'story of power' to describe our view of what power is and how we go about finding it. To find out what yours is, imagine what you'd say to an inquisitive child who asked you to explain what power is. Each person's story determines whether they see power as attractive or attainable. More importantly, it forms the basis for deciding whether a particular goal is within or beyond your power.

When I interviewed Susan, she told me that she was satisfied with most aspects of her life. She was a successful businesswoman with two young children and in her story of power, she had about as much of it as she needed. She felt able to make choices in her life and most of her important goals were within her reach. But she had one area where she felt her power leave her. It was when she watched the news or saw television programmes about the state of the world. She felt concerned for the kind of future her children would face. When describing these fears, she said to me: 'I'm just one small person, what can I do? I feel totally powerless.'

This is a feeling that many of the people I interviewed shared. It is related to a story that sees world issues as beyond the power of ordinary people to influence. The next shift supports a new story of power that can help turn this feeling of powerlessness around.

From big to small

According to Newton's Second Law of Motion, the effect of a force is proportional to its size. A big force has a big effect, a small force has a small effect and a tiny force has such a minuscule effect that for all practical purposes it can be ignored. But what happens when we apply this fundamental law of physics to the realm of personal power? Look at the following statements and see how much you agree with them.

◆ *Making big changes in your life requires a massive amount of effort. Unless you're going to be completely devoted, there's no point in even starting.*
◆ *To influence something huge like the world you need a massive force. If you don't have this, you don't stand much chance.*

The assumption behind both these statements is that to do something big you need something big (for example massive willpower, loads of money or a position of influence). If you haven't got this, you're unlikely to succeed. Newton's Second Law has so entered the unconscious fabric of western thinking that this assumption is often regarded as a statement of fact. The effect of thinking this way is that small steps and individual actions frequently get dismissed as being a waste of time. This can lead people to believe that big changes, whether in their personal lives or the world, are beyond their power.

A recently retired woman on one of my courses told me how this way of thinking blocked action in her life. 'Each time I consider doing something,' she said, 'I think "that won't do much", so I don't bother.' However, advances in science have questioned Newton's Second Law and this has important implications for how we look at power.

In 1979, Edward Lorenz presented a paper about chaos theory[3] to the American Association for the Advancement of Science. The title was: 'Does the flap of a butterfly's wings in Brazil set off a tornado in Texas?'

When Lorenz had been a research meteorologist studying weather patterns, he'd found that altering the initial conditions of a computer weather simulation by a minuscule amount led to huge differences in how the weather turned out. A change in starting point as small as a butterfly flapping its wings could lead to a weather disturbance as big as a tornado. The small change became amplified over time, leading the weather to go off in a completely different track. This way in which tiny changes can have massive consequences is known as the butterfly effect. It is now an accepted finding of modern science.

The butterfly effect and Newton's Second Law of Motion lead to contrasting views about what can happen as a result of a tiny action. When you're poised on the decision of whether or not to do something, these different perspectives can powerfully influence your eventual actions. For example, if a bright idea for a new project pops up in your mind, do you dismiss it as an unrealistic fantasy or decide to take the first step? That first move might be something you can easily do, like make a phone call or write a letter. But it is so easy to dismiss these tiny steps if you think: 'There's no point, it won't make any difference.'

The importance of the butterfly effect is that it offers a perspective that helps you find your power. It is a way of thinking about small actions that makes them significant and worthwhile. Each effort contributes to something larger and it may only be later that you see how a decision made in a moment sets off a sequence of events that leads to much bigger changes.

What we have here is a basis for a new story of power. However, if you've been brought up to believe that tiny actions don't make much difference, you might wonder how the butterfly effect can possibly work. Throughout this book we'll be exploring several of the mechanisms by which small changes can become amplified to create much larger effects. Understanding how this happens allows you to target your actions in a way that can make them more effective. One of these mechanisms is what I call the 'journey effect', and the following example illustrates this at work.

> *Malindi used to be painfully shy. She found it difficult to talk to people and because of this dreaded social gatherings. However, she also hated feeling on the outside of groups. This left her caught in a conflict between the desire to connect with people and her fear of the embarrassment that went with this. One day, she made a decision to tackle her shyness. It had reached the point where she could see that it was making her miserable and she wanted to do something about it. So she started a process of what she called shyness training.*
>
> *One saying she had found helpful was: 'Take small steps from where you are.' She started to challenge her shyness by saying 'hello' to people. It was a tiny step, but sometimes this simple greeting became the beginning of a conversation. Through these conversations, she began to make friends and feel more comfortable talking with others. Five years later, I heard a friend of mine describe Malindi as 'amazingly confident'. That simple decision to tackle shyness had started a journey. Through many steps of courage, Malindi had travelled a huge distance. She had changed so much that it was difficult to believe she used to be shy.*

Malindi's story illustrates the journey effect in the context of personal development. You can apply the same principle to promote change at the level of groups, organizations or our world. The starting point is simply making a decision.

For example, if you feel concerned about an issue, the decision to do something about it starts a ball rolling. Each time you identify a step and take it, you move the journey of change forward. The smaller steps might seem insignificant when looked at by themselves, but they always form part of a bigger picture. When you see how they add up over time, you recognize what they can lead to. This is the approach of *power through*, where you appreciate how larger changes happen through the smaller ones. Whether in changing the world or your life, each tiny step can be built on and further developed; it doesn't have to stop there. The small movements become openings and starting points that can lead to other things.

This next exercise provides an opportunity to apply this in your life. If you get into the habit of doing this every day, you'll be amazed how far it can take you.

> **Try this: Applying the butterfly effect**
> ◆ *What is your call to adventure at the moment? What goal or project feels most important to you?*
> ◆ *If you were to take one step, no matter how small, that would move this forward, what would it be? See what happens if you take that step today.*

One of the positive side effects when people start taking steps in directions that are important to them is that they tend to feel better. This is a reliable way of improving your mood. It also tends to raise your energy. With this new story of power, the emphasis is on identifying the areas you want to address, making a decision to begin the journey of change, and then taking the steps that move you in the direction you want to go.

But how do you find the power to make the changes you want to make? This is where the next shift is important.

From noun to verb

I once counselled a man who used to psychologically torture his wife. He believed that if she were knocked down and undermined, then he would have the power in the relationship. He was viewing power as a thing that only one of them could have. If she had it, then he didn't, so he believed he needed to keep it from her.

When we think of power as a noun like this, it becomes an object that can be accumulated by some and taken from others. This leads to a competitive approach, where one person's gain is seen as someone else's loss. But does it have to be this way?

This book is based on an approach that defines personal power as the ability to move in the direction you want to go. While the word *ability* is a noun, *move* is a verb. Verbs are words that refer to active processes. When you shift the focus from the noun (what people have) to the verb (what people do), you emphasize the action that people are taking. This shift can help turn around the powerlessness we may feel when we don't have the things we associate with power (such as money, weapons or status).

This change in thinking is central to the approach we're exploring: each of the chapters introduces active processes that open up personal power. In this chapter, for example, the action is thinking about power differently.

This action takes place in our mind and it can effectively switch power on.

There will be some tasks that are easily within our power, but we still find difficult to do. I look around at my kitchen. I have the power to tidy it, it is within my capability. The noun form of power isn't enough, though. There needs to be an active principle too. When I ask myself 'How can I power myself to tidy my kitchen?' I start to think in a different way. If I'm feeling resistant to the task, I start planning ways to coax myself into activity. I put a timer on for 20 minutes and do a deal with myself: 'Just 20 minutes, then I'll do something I want to do.' Powering ourselves isn't just about being able to say 'I can'. It also involves the phrase 'I will'. This leads to the next shift.

From 'they should' to 'I will'

The approach of *power over* focuses on how we can get other people to do things. Having this sort of power is about controlling others. But the reality is that we have little control over what other people do. Whatever our role or status, there are always likely to be some people who frustrate us by behaving differently to how we'd like. The danger of focusing too much on their behaviour rather than our own is this: we can get stuck in the role of complaining. While complaint does have a valid role up to a point, the challenge of personal power is to recognize where that point is.

In the last chapter, we looked at how feelings of dissatisfaction can become important motivators for change. This was referred to as inspirational dissatisfaction. One way we become aware of our concerns is when we hear ourselves complaining about them. Forbidding ourselves ever to talk negatively about anything can block the awareness of grievances that need airing as a prelude to dealing with them. Moaning might be the necessary step by which we talk ourselves into tackling an issue. The challenge is to notice when we've been on the same moan for too long. This is the point at which to say: 'From they should to I will.'

Since the person you can influence most is yourself, it makes sense to focus on what you can do. But what if you can't see what to do or you're not sure what you want? This is when you need some tools. The next chapter introduces a powerful strategy for finding your direction and translating bright ideas into action. It is called the dream cycle, and it provides a mechanism for applying the approach to finding your power described in this chapter.

Power Points

The way you think about power can either open it up or close it down. Five shifts in perspective that make power more available and attractive are:

1 **From viewing power as control to seeing it as influence**. Even if a situation is out of your control, you may still be able to influence it. Each of your choices acts like a vote that steers things in a particular direction.

2 **From a view of power based on physics to one from psychology**. You don't need to force yourself or others in order to bring about change. Instead, learn how to stimulate the desire for change, and then seek out the understanding or skills that make it possible.

3 **From a focus on bigness to recognizing the power of tiny steps**. The butterfly effect describes how tiny forces can have huge effects. This perspective reminds you that small actions can and do make a difference.

4 **From viewing power as a noun to seeing it as a verb**. When you shift the focus from noun (what you have) to verb (what you do), you emphasize the active steps you can take to power yourself.

5 **From 'they should' to 'I will'**. When you focus on what you can do rather than on what you think others should do, you move out of complaining and into action. But if you're not sure what to do, the dream cycle introduced in the next chapter can help.

3

Combining Vision with Pragmatism

While the last chapter looked more at the theory side of personal power, this chapter focuses on the practice. It introduces a simple strategy that, with as little as ten minutes' input each day, can significantly improve your ability to move in the directions that are important to you. This strategy is based on the holistic principle that the whole is more than the sum of the parts. By bringing together and integrating elements often seen as opposite, like dreaming and realism, it becomes possible to be both pragmatic and visionary at the same time. I call this strategy the *dream cycle* and I think of it as the engine of personal power.

Realistic optimism

Many years ago I had an argument over lunch with one of my professors. He said: 'Dreaming is a waste of time, we need to be pragmatic.' I replied: 'Dreaming is what inspires us to better things, to bring positive changes into our lives and the world.' We didn't convince each other, because we had both got locked into defending our positions. But I can see now how we were both right in different ways.

When we have a vision that inspires us, it gives us a direction to head in and this can be energizing. But it is also possible to get lost in dreams in a way that detaches us from reality. As Professor Dumbledore warns in the first Harry Potter[1] story: 'It does not do to dwell on dreams and forget to live.'

What we explore in this chapter is a way of being grounded in present reality while also taking active steps towards the dreams that inspire you. We will be using the approach of 'realistic optimism', defined by performance coaches Jim Loehr and Tony Schwartz[2] as:

> *a paradoxical notion that implies seeing the world as it is, but always working positively towards a desired outcome or solution.*

Although dreams and reality are sometimes seen as opposites, it is more helpful to think of them as two points in a journey. Present reality is the starting point of where you are now. Dream, goal and vision are different words to describe the places you want to get to. Personal power is what helps you move from where you are to where you want to be (see Figure 3.1).

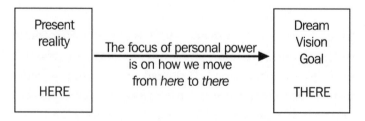

Figure 3.1 Dreams and reality

The term 'dream' is sometimes used in a way that implies the destination is beyond your reach, for example when someone dismisses a proposal as 'just a dream'. In this book I'm using dream to refer to the things you most want to happen. Whether that's beyond your reach or not doesn't just depend on where the destination is. It also depends on how determined you are to get there, and what tools you have to deal with any obstacles in the way. This is where personal power makes a difference, as the following example illustrates.

Susie came on one of my courses because she was feeling lost. She wanted to do something useful with her life, which involved activities she enjoyed and earned her enough money to meet her needs. This was her dream. But she didn't have a clear vision of what this work might be or how to move towards it.

As we explored this, it became clear that Susie was dismissing any option that would take her more than two years to reach. She regarded these as too ambitious, as 'just dreaming'. As none of the remaining choices excited her, she was left feeling aimless and without direction.

The breakthrough for Susie came when she began to think in longer time frames and consider what she really wanted to be doing in five or ten years' time. In allowing herself to dream, she got a clearer image of the sort of future that attracted her. She pictured herself taking groups of young people out climbing or on outdoor activities. She loved this idea and started to think about training as a climbing instructor. By the end of the course, her level of energy had soared. She had found a purpose.

It isn't so much what the goal *is* but what the goal *does* that is important. Although the destination may be in the future, the effect it can have is very much in the present. When we have something to aim for, this mobilizes our energy. But as well as having a goal, we also need to have some confidence that we might be able to reach it.

Susie told me that before my course she hadn't had the tools needed to plot a path towards distant goals. Having a dream but not seeing how to achieve it was depressing, and so she'd stopped herself thinking about goals she saw as ambitious. 'The course tooled me up,' she said. It gave her psychological tools that helped translate her dreams for the future into practical action steps in the present. One of these tools was the dream cycle.

The dream cycle

When I enter a new situation, the first thing I do is look around and review what's happening. Having got a measure of things, I ask myself: 'What would I like to happen here?' Once I have a sense of my desired outcome, I consider what I can do to move in that direction. If I've identified a step, I need to take it. Sometimes it works out, sometimes it doesn't. Either way, I look at what happened as a result of what I did.

What I've described here is a series of steps that includes reviewing, visioning, planning, taking action and then reviewing again. These may be things we intuitively do without much thought. What the dream cycle does is build on what we naturally do by giving each of these steps more conscious focus. It is a navigation tool that can be used to help us steer ourselves more towards the things we do want and away from what we don't want.

Some people seem to have a natural talent for dreaming up new projects, others are reflective and draw out lessons from the past. There are those who give great attention to planning, while some other people just get on with things. If you have a team, it is good to have the right balance of these different strengths. When you're looking at your own life, you need all of them. For example, if you only focus on getting things done without reviewing whether this is leading you where you want to go, you risk making excellent progress – in the wrong direction.

In a similar way, for dreaming to be useful it needs to be followed by the sort of practical planning that identifies achievable next steps. What the dream cycle does is bring together these four different elements of Dream, Plan, Do and Review. Each is like a piece of a jigsaw: incomplete by itself, but able to play a vital role when integrated into a larger structure (see Figure 3.2).

Figure 3.2 Dream, Plan, Do, Review – the dream cycle

You can use this process over a range of time frames. For example, you could go round the cycle in a day, or even in an hour, or use it when looking at a week, month, year, decade or your life as a whole. If it were to be applied to a single day, you might begin soon after waking by spending a few moments reviewing what's going on in your life and what's important to you within it. You then move into the dream phase by imagining what kind of day you would like to have. Planning might involve asking yourself what you can do to make such a day more likely to happen.

When you identify specific steps that can make a difference, you open up your power to shape the day ahead. What I've just described here is the short form of the dream cycle (see Figure 3.3). It can take just a few minutes in a morning, but has the potential to change the way you approach the whole day.

Figure 3.3 The short form of the dream cycle

Being a circular process, the dream cycle is designed to be repeated often. This allows you to adjust to changing circumstances. For example, if by lunchtime it becomes clear that your original plans are unworkable, you can pause to Review what's happening. The Dream phase involves considering what you'd like to happen in what is left of the day, and Plan focuses on what you can do to make your desired outcome more likely to happen. Then it is back to the Do phase.

The longer the time period you're looking at, the more attention it's worth giving to each stage. If you've looked at what you most want from your life as a whole, it becomes easier to work out how to approach the next decade. This in turn makes the next year clearer. If you have clarity about your goals for the year, then what you do in each day can become a step towards these. Through doing this, the little steps become aligned with, and contribute to, the bigger purposes that are important to you. This gives your life a much clearer sense of direction. There is also evidence that it could make you happier. Here's why.

Flow experiences

The research on happiness suggests that people tend to be at their most content when they are engaged in what psychologists call a 'flow experience'. These are the moments when we're so completely absorbed in what we're doing that we lose track of time.

Psychologist Mihaly Czikszentmihalyi,[3] who has spent decades researching into what makes people happiest, writes:

The best moments usually occur when a person's body or mind is stretched to its limits in a voluntary effort to accomplish something difficult and worthwhile.

Flow experiences are most likely to occur when we're engaged in a task that is challenging enough to require some level of skill and effort, but also not so hard that we feel defeated by it. We tend to feel in flow when we are able to concentrate on a clear goal that we have a reasonable chance of achieving. Many games or sports are attractive because they generate flow experiences, but only if we're playing at a level appropriate to our abilities. If it's too easy it becomes boring, but if it's too demanding we can feel anxious, overwhelmed or out of our depth.

One of the advantages of thinking about our life goals is that it makes it possible to turn more of our everyday living into a flow experience. Each day presents us with the task, challenge and opportunity of moving in the direction we most want to go. The dream cycle provides a structure for regularly reviewing goals and progress towards them, so that we can make the adjustments necessary to more fully and easily enter into our flow. For example, if current goals appear too difficult, these can be revised or the planning stage used to problem solve and identify achievable next steps.

While the short form can be used on a daily basis, it is worth taking a more in-depth approach at regular intervals. Significant birthdays, ends of year and changes of season all offer natural pause points to reflect on where you are, where you want to go and how you might get there. Looking at each stage of the dream cycle in turn, the following pages offer techniques for enhancing this process.

Review

When you're reviewing, you're looking around and asking yourself questions on the theme of: 'What's happening?' The aim is to get an accurate perception of current reality. This involves looking as honestly as you can at whatever is going on. As the saying goes: 'In order to get to where you want to go, you need to start from where you are.' With the review stage you're getting clear where that is. The following five questions are useful starting points for this.

What do I feel good about?

If you're going to look at any difficult areas, you can put yourself in a better position to do this by first developing a positive frame of mind. Research[4] has shown that problem-solving abilities are improved when people are in a good mood. One way to develop this is simply to give your attention to the things you feel good about. It has been shown that spending a few minutes every day identifying events in the last 24 hours that you feel thankful for can significantly boost your levels of joy and happiness.[5]

When you look for the things you've done that you feel good about, you open up a way of building your confidence. In a review exercise, a participant at one of my courses was surprised at how many things like this she had done in the last two weeks. 'I would never have noticed all of these unless I'd specifically looked, but seeing them like this gives me the feeling that I am moving forward after all,' she said. Doing this had helped her shift from feeling that she was stuck. See what happens when you do this.

> **Try this: Noticing the positives**
> Write a list of all the things you've done (no matter
> how small) in the last two weeks that you feel good
> about.

Savouring successes, both big and small ones, is a way of
strengthening positive belief in yourself. This helps prepare you for the next part of review: taking in a clear view
of whatever is happening.

What's happening here?

The dream cycle is a tool that can be applied to any area
and this second question invites you to take an overview
of current conditions. Whether you're looking at a relationship, your finances, your health or your life as a
whole, it is useful to start with a wide-angle view that recognizes both the good and not so good aspects of the situation. So to begin, choose what you want to look at.
Whatever this is, ask yourself: 'What's happening here?'

In the simple act of looking, you take power.
Awareness is the first stage of engagement and by itself
can be an effective tool for change. When I interviewed
Elisabeth, a busy single parent, she told me: 'Whenever I
look at my finances, I make money.' Because this was an
area she didn't feel confident in, she had tended to avoid
looking. By reviewing, she became aware of areas where
she could save money; if she was spending too much, this
was part of how she brought herself back on track.

If there is so much happening in an area that you feel
overwhelmed or stressed when you look at it, using projective techniques can help. These allow you to quickly
pour out whatever is on your mind onto somewhere
where you can more easily look at it. When your head is

too full, it can be a great relief to do this. Writing, drawing, mind maps or other forms of expression can be used. Here's a simple way of doing this.

> ### Review technique 1: The bubblegram
> First choose an area you want to look at, then ask yourself: 'What's happening here?'
> On different parts of a blank piece of paper, write down the items as they pop up in your mind, putting a circle around each one. This is a useful way of mapping out different elements of a situation so that you get an overview of things as a whole.

What feelings do I have here?

Review involves listening inside as well as looking outside. Feelings give information about your level of satisfaction with each area, and also draw attention to issues that might require attention. If you're not sure what you're feeling, writing or talking can be a useful way of becoming clearer.

It is common for emotions to lie just beneath the surface of awareness, only to emerge when given space to express themselves. I've often heard people say: 'I didn't realize I felt so strongly about this until I heard myself talking about it.' It is similar with writing: filling a page with words can be a way of pouring out the content of your mind or heart onto somewhere you can more easily look at it.

Here is another projective technique for doing this.

Review technique 2: Writing open-ended sentences

Start a sentence with the words 'I feel...' or 'Feelings I have include...' and see what naturally follows. Just let the words fall out, whatever wants to come. When you run out of things to say, start the sentence again and see if anything else comes.

Each time you begin a sentence like this, the opening phrase can act as a starting-off point for a new avenue of expression. It is common to have a number of different feelings at the same time, so by repeating the sentence you give yourself an opportunity to explore the range of emotions around for you.

While in the past this sort of listening to yourself may have been regarded as self-indulgent navel gazing, it is now increasingly recognized as a vital step in developing emotional intelligence. For example, Harvard Business School offers courses in self-reflection for businesspeople and professionals, and there is a growing body of research[6] showing the importance of emotions in decision making.

You can develop emotional self-awareness by the simple practice of noticing your reactions to events. When you become aware of your heart racing in response to a piece of news, it tells you something. It is a marker of significance. In a similar way, would you go ahead with a decision if you felt in your guts that it was wrong? Our feelings can alert us to the need to give something our attention. This leads to the next question.

What needs my attention?
The easiest way to find out what needs your attention is
to ask yourself this question, then listen quietly and see
what answer comes. Often we know what we need to do.
But it is when we stop and listen to ourselves that this has
a chance to move from the back of our minds to the front.

The question 'What needs my attention?' can provoke
an avalanche of responses. If you have more crying out for
your attention than you have attention to give, then it is a
good time to remember the parsnip story. Many years ago
I worked as a gardener. My task one spring day was to
murder parsnip seedlings. There were rows of them and
they looked beautiful. But for every eight seedlings, only
one could stay. When I'm flooded with demands for my
attention, I remember the parsnips. They could only
grow big enough to eat if they had plenty of space around
them. That's why the thinning out was necessary. Each
project is like a seedling. For it to develop well, it needs
the space to grow. We only have room for so many things
at a time. The following technique applies this thinning-
out approach to personal planning.

Review technique 3: Saying yes means saying no
If you find yourself overloaded with demands for
your attention, list them all. Think of your list as sim-
ilar to an unruly garden that needs thinning out.

As you go down the list, ask yourself: 'What
would happen if I didn't do this?' If more would be
gained than lost, then consider letting that item go.
Each task you choose to abandon frees up attention
for what really matters. Saying yes (to what matters)
means saying no (to what matters less). Saying no is
therefore part of saying yes.

The big question is: 'What do you most want to say yes to?' This leads to the next area of review.

What really matters here?
A core function of reviewing is to help you notice when you're drifting away from what's important to you, so that you can bring yourself back on course. Central to this is getting clear about what matters to you most. It is useful to consider two areas here: destinations and values. *Destinations* are about where you're aiming to get to, in terms of the goals and purposes you set yourself. *Values* are your beliefs about what you consider most important.

It is your values that determine which destinations you think of as worthwhile, and also what methods you find acceptable in order to reach them. Your values therefore act as the inner compass that helps you to find your course. Whenever you're feeling lost or unclear, coming back to the question 'What really matters here?' can be a step towards finding your way.

Focusing on what's important to you is a way of increasing your level of engagement and energy. There's a problem, though, when you find yourself caught between competing values that matter. This is a common cause of stress. When I worked as a family doctor, I often felt squeezed between the values of speed and thoroughness. It was important to be thorough so that I didn't make mistakes, but if I took too much time I wouldn't be able to see all the people waiting for me.

In some situations, like with the parsnips, it is important to make choices between areas. But there are also times, like in my medical practice, when it isn't so much about choosing as about finding the right balance between competing values. The way to find this balance is by noticing the times it isn't there, and then looking at what you can do to correct this.

Noticing imbalance is essentially a feeling or emotional response. Something feels wrong when the balance isn't there. But to change this we need to move into the next part of the cycle – to consider how you would like things to be. This is the dream phase. Before moving into it, try the following review exercise.

Try this: Identifying what really matters
◆ *What are the things that matter to you most? (A bubblegram may help.)*
◆ *How satisfied do you feel with the current balance of these things in your life?*

Dream

Dreaming is a word that has negative associations for some people. It may be seen as the opposite of being realistic or pragmatic. When this happens, it is usually much to do with the way that dreaming is being looked at, seeing it in isolation rather than as part of a larger creative process. As a solitary piece of a jigsaw it isn't enough, but as part of the dream cycle it becomes a practical step in making things happen.

With review you look at where you are and where you've been; with the dream stage you look at where you want to go. As Albert Einstein once said: 'Your imagination offers a preview of life's coming attractions.'

Many people on my courses tell me: 'I don't know what my dream is.' They may not have a clear target for their life as a whole, but they are usually pretty clear about their preferences. There are some things that they would definitely not like to happen, and other things that they would like. Your *don't wants* tell you what you want to avoid or move away from, your *wants* give you something to steer towards.

For example, if someone doesn't have a clear sense of direction but would like one, then finding a purpose becomes their goal. We could call this a 'stepping-stone' dream – although it may not be the ultimate dream, it is a step that takes them in the direction they want to go. This is all about navigation, where having a destination to head for gives your life purpose and direction. This focuses your energy in a way that opens up personal power.

So how do you find your dream or purpose? Here again, you can use projective techniques.

> **Try this: Day dreaming**
> Close your eyes and imagine yourself watching a film that's called 'The dreams or goals that most excite me include...' What do you see?
>
> **Try this: Postcard from your dreams**
> On a blank postcard or piece of paper, draw your dreams and deepest desires. You don't need to think too much about it, just let your hand doodle and see what comes. Use different colours, and allow yourself to become absorbed.

When you use techniques like these, you draw out your deeper motivations. Identifying goals that touch your heart is of central importance to finding your power. Only there's a problem that often occurs when you do this. Part of the mind that I think of as 'the editor' usually starts pointing out the reasons why your dream is a bad idea. 'Sounds nice, but I can't see that happening' it might say. As each delightful image gets shot down, you can easily end up like Susie before she came on my course. She felt aimless because she'd dismissed all the aims that felt worthwhile to her.

In order to mobilize the inspirational energy that your dreams can evoke, it is necessary, at least temporarily, to bypass the inner editor. One of the ways you can do this is by using the 'wild question' technique.

What would you do if you were free from fear and knew that you could not fail? A question like this allows you to see through the anxiety and disbelief that so often block out inspired vision. There are other questions that serve this purpose too. Here are some examples:

◆ *What would you do if you won a fortune on the lottery tomorrow?*
◆ *What have you always wanted to do but held yourself back from?*
◆ *If you were granted three wishes that you knew would come true, how would you use them?*

I call these wild questions because they invite you to think outside your normal limitations. They counter the part of the brain that says: 'I can't do that because...' There will always be reasons why you can't or shouldn't do something. But if you let these stop you even considering what you want, motivational energy gets cut off at its source.

The dream cycle focuses on the *what* before the *how*. Dreaming is about identifying what you'd like to happen, and then the planning stage explores how you might move in that direction.

Wild questions sometimes involve the use of magic, for example being offered three wishes. At first this might seem to be encouraging you to think unrealistically. But how many of today's marvels, like laptop computers, would have been regarded as magic 100 years ago? Something seems magical when you can't see how it can be done. As soon as you find a way, you become able to do things that previously you might have thought of as magical.

So when you're facing an obstacle that seems impossible to pass, imagine what might happen if you were to learn new ways of dealing with blocks. Knowing what you really want is the starting point of the journey of personal power. It is your call to adventure. So with this in mind, see what comes up when you try the following exercise.

> **Try this: The magic self-help book**
> You read a magic self-help book that mysteriously gives you the power to achieve any goal, dream or ambition. What would you choose to do?

Don't be put off if, at the moment, your goal seems impossibly far away. There are tools in the chapters ahead that can help you. Just for now, consider what it would be like if it were possible.

As Paulo Coelho[7] writes in his bestselling book *The Alchemist*: 'It's the possibility of having a dream come true that makes life interesting.' The next stage takes a practical look at how you start bringing that possibility into being.

Plan

There are two sides to the meaning of the word plan: one is intention; the other is working out how to do things. For example, if you've decided to do something, you might say: 'I plan to...' This is a statement of intention. However, if you're really serious about it, you become involved in the idea. You start thinking about how to do it, working out details and problem solving any difficulties that stand in the way. This is the second part.

Intention
It is one thing to know what you want. It is another to make a decision to go for it. Making a decision like this is one of the ways in which you power yourself.

Below is a process for making and strengthening the kind of decision that powerful intentions grow out of. I call it the intentioning process. It has four stages.

The intentioning process

STAGE 1: IDENTIFY YOUR DESIRED DESTINATION
Start by asking yourself: 'What do I really want? What is the goal or dream that I want to move towards?'

Identify one specific target that you'd really like to reach.

STAGE 2: TASTE THE DREAM
Close your eyes and imagine you are actually there. You have arrived.

How does it feel? What colours do you see? What smells do you notice? What are the best bits? And the worst? You are exploring in your mind how it feels to have your dream come true.

After tasting the dream like this, ask yourself if this is something you really want to head towards. If it isn't, wait until you have a dream you feel more positive about, and then start the process again.

STAGE 3: HOW IMPORTANT IS THIS TO YOU?
Facing a difficult challenge requires courage, determination, effort and the risk that you might lose things you value in the process of moving towards your goal. The third stage is to ask yourself how important this goal is to you.

If it isn't important, it may not be worth the effort. But if it is, why is that?

If you have good reasons, this strengthens your will and deepens your determination. Even if you can't quite see how you are going to get there, if you have the will, you are more likely to find the way.

STAGE 4: MAKE A DECISION AND A COMMITMENT
If this dream is both important and attractive to you, the next stage is to make a clear decision to head towards it. That decision needs to be backed up by a commitment to take the steps needed to move you the way you want to go. For example, writing down your decision and your goal is a way of showing to yourself that you are serious about this, that you are committed.

Does it seem a bit forward to commit yourself before you know how to reach your goal? This is one of the key shifts that opens up personal power. If you only commit to goals that you already know how to reach, you limit yourself to doing what you already know how to do. But when you make a decision to head for a new destination, you start a journey that turns your life into an adventure. The commitment you make is to taking the steps, to acting on your serious intention to reach your goal. What you're doing with this is planting the seeds of your dream in the reality of the present.

An important aspect of the intentioning process is seeing yourself succeeding. If you can picture yourself arriving at your destination, then you have already taken a significant step towards it. Visualizing yourself doing something is a form of preparation: referred to as mental rehearsal, it has become an accepted and proven method of enhancing performance. The other side of this is that if you can't see yourself doing something, then it is worth exploring what's in the way of this.

Because the dream cycle is a cyclical process, if you use it regularly you will find yourself coming back to this intentioning process again and again. Intentions need to be reinforced repeatedly if they are to maintain their potency. You can do this by periodically revisiting your decision and, if you still want to head towards it, recommitting to your goal. Each time you remind yourself why something is important to you, you feed and strengthen your intention in a way that helps it grow. However, once you have a strong intention you will also want to act on this. This leads to the second part of the planning process: working out the practical details of how to move towards your desired destination.

Working out how
When I interviewed John, he told me that he didn't like to plan things, because he wanted to be open to each

moment and stay in the present. When we explored this further, two things became clear. First, there were some disadvantages to living a life that was too highly planned. A plan involves making decisions in the present about what you might do at a point in the future. But come that future time, you might want to do something different. Being tied to a plan can limit freedom.

However, the second thing that became clear was that John was frustrated with his life. He lacked a clear sense of direction and felt bored with much of what he did. Because of his avoidance of planning, he had excluded himself from the more complex and challenging goals that might have inspired him.

Planning involves thinking about something before it happens, in a way that allows you to prepare for it. The two core questions are: 'Where do I want to get to?' and 'What do I need in order to do this?' Although this may sound obvious, effective planning skills are rarely taught in schools and it is common for people to run into problems that could have been avoided with better planning. Have you had the experience of running into trouble halfway through a project because you hadn't thought of an essential detail beforehand? I certainly have. Such things are always easier to see after they've happened, and when I slip up like this, I'm aware of that scolding voice inside me that says: 'Why didn't I think of that before?' The good news is that we can use the benefit of hindsight like this to plan for future goals.

If you pretend that the occasion you're planning for has already happened, then you can look back in time from an imaginary point in the future. If you do this, you can use imaginary hindsight to see those things that are easier to see after they have happened. Research[8] has shown that when people use this technique, they are better at working out how events can occur. They also tend to give more detailed descriptions of how challenges are faced and dealt with.

When you're wondering how to do something, rather than asking 'How can I do this?' imagine that you have already succeeded, picture yourself there, then ask yourself how you did it.

Try this: Imaginary hindsight

◆ *Focus your attention on a goal you would like to achieve.*

◆ *Pretend for a moment that you have succeeded. Picture yourself there in that imaginary future where it has worked out the way you want it to.*

◆ *Now tell the story of how it occurred. Make sure you include a clear description of any decisions you made, help you sought or new skills you developed. How did you manage it?*

At this stage, you don't need a precise blueprint. What you're doing is giving your attention to possible pathways and necessary preparation. By looking back in time from an imaginary future, you're looking in a different way that helps you see things you hadn't noticed before.

Another way of getting a fresh perspective is to ask someone else. The most valuable people to ask are those who've already succeeded in doing what you want to do (or something close to it). If you're planning to travel somewhere new, speak to someone who's been there. If you want to learn a new skill, find a person who can do it already. We learn so much by modelling and sharing experience – we don't need to reinvent the wheel each time.

The final point of any planning needs to be identifying your next step. The more specific you are about exactly what you're going to do and when you're going to do it, the more likely you are to succeed. If a goal is vague, it can float. To bring it to ground it needs to be anchored by detail. For example, in a study[9] looking at factors encouraging non-exercising students to join a fitness programme, the rates of those taking part rose from 39 to 91 per cent simply through asking them to identify when and where they intended to exercise.

When you have a project that you want to take forward but you're not sure how, I invite you to use the following process. I first learnt it over 16 years ago at a workshop with Joanna Macy,[10] a writer and teacher known internationally for her work helping people find their power to tackle world issues. I have adapted it so that it can be used for both personal and planetary purposes. Either way, this exercise can be remarkably effective at boiling big dreams down to specific next steps.

The action planning process

This exercise guides you through seven questions. You can use it alone, exploring responses in your journal. You can also use it with a partner or friend, taking it in turns to interview and encourage each other.

◆ *If you knew you could not fail, what dream would you most like to pursue?*

◆ *What specific goal can you realistically aim to achieve in the next 12 months that would contribute towards this?*

◆ *What strengths and resources do you already have that can help you succeed in this?*

◆ *What strengths and resources do you still need to develop in order to reach your goal?*

◆ *How might you sabotage yourself?*

◆ *How will you find a way of countering this?*

◆ *What can you do in the next 24 hours, no matter how small a step, that will move you towards your goal?*

Once you've identified your next action step, you're ready to move out of planning and into the next phase of the dream cycle. Do!

Do

Try this: Take a step

If you were to identify a small, positive, achievable step that would move you towards your chosen goal, what would it be?

Why not go ahead and do that right now?

The 'do' stage is where you just get on with it. However, if you're finding it difficult to get started, the following start-up strategies can help. Like an athlete running up to a jump, we sometimes need to physically and/or psychologically mobilize energy in order to more easily spring into action. I think of this as taking the step before the step. The next page shows three ways of doing this.

Start-up strategy 1: Make your target near and clear

If you're stalling, it could be because your goal either isn't clear enough or seems too difficult. Is there an easier and better-defined first step you can take that starts the journey?

Start-up strategy 2: Just five minutes

A way of making a task more achievable is to tell yourself you only have to do it for five minutes and then review. Set a timer. Any task becomes less daunting if you only have to do it for a short while, and once you've taken the first step it is often easier to continue.

Start-up strategy 3: Do it now!

Once you've a clear target in mind, just say the words 'Do it now!' and do it. Keep repeating those words until you find yourself moving.

If you've recently taken a step, congratulations. But if you haven't, why not try one of the start-up strategies above. Just put the book down and think of the butterfly effect: one tiny step can make a difference. It could be a phone call, the washing-up, a page of writing or a simple exercise routine. So long as it moves you, even if only a tiny bit, in a direction important to you, that's all that's needed.

If you're not yet ready to move into the action phase, that's fine too. But it is worth exploring what might be needed in order to become ready. This is the sort of thing to look at in the review stage, which you've now come back to.

Review (again)

How did you get on? When you review your actions, you give yourself a chance to fine-tune them. Each time you go round the cycle there is opportunity for learning. But you are also checking your course, ensuring that the journey you're on really is the one you want to be on.

So – what do you feel good about? There will always be something if you look for it, and doing this can boost both mood and confidence. Then look at what you can learn. If you didn't succeed in doing what you hoped, you may have picked up some information that can improve your chances next time round.

This cycle is a perpetual process, like a bicycle wheel that, with each rotation, transports you further in the way you want to go. However, to both start and continue this process you need to be reasonably confident that it will be worth the effort. How do you develop the trust and strength of confidence that enable you to keep going even through the difficult times? This is what we look at in the next chapter.

Power Points

1 Although dreams and reality are sometimes seen as opposites, it is more helpful to think of them as two points on a journey. Present reality is your starting point; your dream tells you where you'd like to get to.

2 The dream cycle brings together the elements of Dream, Plan, Do and Review. Each is like a piece of a jigsaw,

incomplete in itself, but able to play a vital role when integrated as part of a larger whole.

3 In order to get to where you want to go, you need to start
from where you are. With the review stage you're getting
clear where that is. Awareness is the first stage of engagement and by itself can be an effective tool for change.

4 There will always be reasons why you can't do something.
But if you let these stop you even considering what you'd
like, motivational energy gets cut off at its source. First identify what you'd really like, then work out how to move that
way.

5 It is one thing to know what you want. It is another to make
a decision to go for it. You power yourself by making a clear
decision to move in a particular direction. When you have a
clear target, this mobilizes your energy.

6 Each time you remind yourself why something is important to you, you feed and strengthen your intention in a way that helps it grow.

7 If you're stalling, it could be because your goal either isn't clear enough or seems too difficult. Making your goal near and clear ensures that the next step is achievable.

4

Developing Trust and Confidence

Robbie was nearly a decade sober. It was remarkable to see how she had changed since her treatment for alcoholism all those years ago. However, recently things had gone horribly wrong. Becoming ill with severe arthritis, she had lost her job. 'I thought I was on the scrap heap,' she said, telling me how she had felt being alone, at home, in pain. I asked her how she had kept her sobriety through this difficult time. 'I trusted the process,' she said, 'I could see other people change, and I thought if they could do it, then maybe so could I.' Through her involvement with the self-help group Alcoholics Anonymous, Robbie had watched other alcoholics turn their lives around and find ways through difficult times. She recognized a process of recovery that involved facing and surviving through the storms. Trusting this process gave her strength when she needed it most.

In this chapter we look at how you can develop the confidence needed to stay true to your course even through bumpy times. Part of this involves learning to trust the process in a way that opens it up as a source of strength and personal power. The chapter introduces an approach that can help you do this. It is called process thinking.

Seeing a bigger picture in time

In these days of fast computers and push-button technology, power is often associated with speed and the ability to get rapid results. But what about those actions that seem to have no immediate effect? When you start exercising but your weight remains the same or you write a letter of protest but nothing changes, it is easy to feel that you are wasting your time. After all, what is the point of taking a step when you don't see a measurable benefit from it?

In order to believe that our actions are worthwhile even when they don't bring immediate results, we need a way of looking that can see a bigger picture in time. This is what process thinking is about. It views the present moment as part of a larger, evolving sequence of events. When you look this way, you recognize how small, seemingly insignificant steps feed into and create larger processes of change. Instead of dismissing an action with the thought 'that won't do any good', you entertain the possibility that it could be a step on the way to somewhere you want to go.

Process thinking, as you can see, builds on the butterfly effect introduced in Chapter 2. With this perspective, tiny steps become worth taking even if you're not certain where they will lead. Some processes unfold mysteriously in front of us, in ways that we can't predict. An example from Robbie's life illustrates this.

In a corner of Robbie's front room was an old computer she had hardly touched. She didn't think of herself as the sort of person who understood computers, but she was committed to the process of her recovery. One of the ideas Robbie had picked up from Alcoholics Anonymous was 'look for the positives in each day'. Perhaps being stuck at home was an opportunity to learn how to use that machine.

She enrolled on a computer course. It was a step. 'I realized I wasn't that thick,' she told me, adding how doing this had given her the confidence later to enrol on a counselling course. This was something she'd wanted to do for years, but had never previously thought herself capable of.

If we were to imagine ourselves watching a film of Robbie's life, we wouldn't be able to predict later events reliably just from watching some of the earlier scenes. A story is a process: it is something that evolves and develops over time, often in unexpected ways and with surprise turnarounds. Our lives are like this too: one thing leads to another and we can't know with any certainty what will happen later on just from looking at how things are at the moment. If we accept that we don't know for sure what will happen, then it becomes harder to dismiss hopes and dreams for the future as impossible. This is a great antidote to one of the main blockers of personal power – static thinking.

Static thinking

Static thinking is a way of looking at the world based on the assumption that reality is something fixed and solid. This view is a potent blocker of personal power, as it leads to a belief that you can't really change things. Whether you're looking at personality, deeply ingrained habits, political structures or human nature, this perspective sees the world as similar to a picture hanging on a wall – something that is set in a particular way and can't be altered (see Figure 4.1). If something isn't already in the picture then it just isn't going to happen – and if you don't like it, tough!

Figure 4.1 A picture of reality from the perspective of static thinking

Static thinking and process thinking are two different ways of understanding the nature of reality. One views the world as fixed and solid, while the other regards everything as in a flow of continuous change. Both perspectives can be thought of as correct, in that they both, in different ways, fit with our experience.

For example, in my study I have a big wooden desk. Every time I go into that room, my desk looks exactly the same. It is fixed and solid and isn't suddenly going to turn into anything else. But if I ask myself what that desk looked like 50 years ago, the image in my mind is of a tree. And in 50 years' time, the desk might still be a desk, or a pile of ash scattered in the wind, or it may have gone rotten and decomposed. By widening the time frame, I see movement from one thing to another, whereas within a shorter time frame I am more likely to see things as fixed and solid.

It is similar with a roll of movie film. If you look at consecutive frames, they seem like identical snapshots side by side. But they aren't the same. There are tiny changes from one frame to the next, in a way that adds up over time to create the movement we see when watching the film. Static thinking is like a snapshot where everything seems fixed; process thinking adds the dimension of time to create a moving picture. Movement is created by lots of tiny changes.

When we understand this, it is easier to recognize how seemingly insignificant choices made every day can contribute to a larger process of change. Each little step towards your dreams (see Figure 4.2) makes something that initially seems impossible become more realistic.

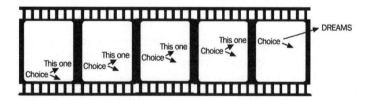

Figure 4.2 Each moment is like a frame in a movie

Self-fulfilling prophecies

At a recent course I was running, several people described having the same problem. They were good at starting things but found it difficult to keep going. One young woman had set up a successful business that she had given up after a few years. She said: 'This is the way I am. I'm no good at sticking with things. This makes me feel unwilling to commit myself to anything new because I'm scared I'm not going to see it through.'

She was taking a static thinking approach to herself, with a self-image that labelled herself as a quitter. The problem with this way of thinking is that it becomes a self-fulfilling prophecy. If you think that you're built a certain way and that you can't change (see Figure 4.3), then you're never likely to take the steps that could prove this idea wrong.

Figure 4.3 A self-portrait from the perspective of static thinking

If you believe you're a quitter, then when you come to a difficult time, you're more likely to give up than perse-vere. Each time someone gives up at something, they strengthen the belief that they are a quitter. The belief and the behaviour reinforce each other, creating a vicious cycle that destroys confidence.

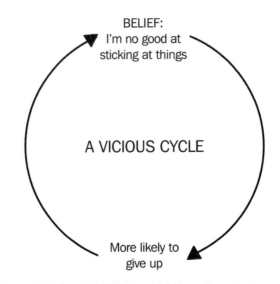

Figure 4.4 A self-fulfilling prophecy of pessimism

Process thinking is useful here because it offers a way out of the vicious cycle shown in Figure 4.4. In fact, it makes it possible to turn the cycle around and get it running the other way. If you start from the assumption that any belief about yourself is a statement about how things are at the moment, rather than how they will be in the future, you open up the possibility of change. The current situation is just one frame in a larger unfolding process. The important questions are: 'Which way do I want to go?' and 'How can I take steps to move in that direction?'

Robbie hadn't thought of herself as the sort of person who understood computers. But she challenged that belief by enrolling on a computer course. 'I realized that I wasn't that thick after all,' she said as she let go of an old limiting belief about herself. This helped her take the next step of enrolling on a counselling course. Each time she took a step like this, it strengthened her belief that positive change was possible. As the strength of this belief grew, so did her confidence to take the next step. This created a positive cycle of recovery where the idea that it is possible to change also became a self-fulfilling prophecy (see Figure 4.5).

BELIEF:
It is possible to change

A POSITIVE CYCLE
OF RECOVERY

Take a step in
self-development

Figure 4.5 A self-fulfilling prophecy of optimism

Personal evolution

Evolution isn't just something seen over millions of years when one species develops into another. It can happen in our lives too, as we move from one version of ourselves into another. We don't have to change our DNA structure in order to open up new abilities – much can be achieved through making a conscious choice to develop ourselves. This is conscious evolution, where we become active participants in a continuing process of change.

Tools like the dream cycle can be used to guide us through this. An even simpler tool is periodically to ask four questions:

◆ *What do I really want?*
◆ *How can I take steps towards this?*
◆ *What gets in the way?*
◆ *How can I deal with that?*

I call these the personal power questions, because just by asking them you can power yourself. The starting point is knowing the direction you want to move in and the first question helps you find this. When you apply this question to yourself, it can be rephrased as 'What do I really want to become?' or 'How do I really want to be?' With the answers to these, you're identifying an ideal you'd like to head towards. The second question starts you on the journey of moving that way. But if you're not sure how to do that, then the next step is to look at what gets in the way. This brings you face to face with whatever is blocking your path.

The advantage of a process thinking approach is that it sees obstacles as just part of the journey. We gain inner strength through facing these difficulties and finding ways through them. It is the process of doing this that strengthens us. This leads to a positive way of looking at confusion, failure and disappointment. These are seen as steps, sometimes even necessary steps, along the way. The concept of stages is useful here.

Something that evolves and changes over time can be seen to move through different stages. For example, a butterfly starts as an egg, then becomes a caterpillar, then retreats from the world for a period while it pupates, after this finally emerging as a butterfly (see Figure 4.6).

Figure 4.6 Stages

But what if one stage were seen as unpleasant? For example, what if the caterpillar thought that being a pupa looked really boring and so it tried to do all it could to avoid going through that phase? Of course caterpillars can't do that, but we can. Quite often we see some phases of development as less attractive than others and so we resist them.

Confusion is a good example of this. In order to grow in understanding we need to allow ourselves to become confused. Why? When we move into new ground and come across something unfamiliar, we're not used to it. It is confusing. It can take us a while to get the hang of it.

If we stick with this confusion phase rather than giving up, things usually become clearer and we then move to a new level of knowledge. We have made a jump. But for that to happen, we need to be willing to enter the confusion zone, in order to move through it into deepened understanding.

Whenever you step into new ground and feel unsure what's going on, remind yourself of this: if you always stay with what you know, you never grow. Confusion is part of the journey on the way to reaching new understanding (see Figure 4.7). Seeing the value of uncertainty like this makes it easier to tolerate. You can take the same approach when facing failure, crisis and disbelief.

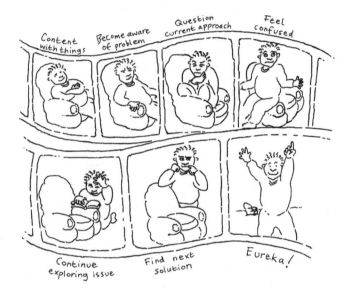

Figure 4.7 Confusion is a stage in the process of learning

The phase of disbelief

A journalist friend of mine described the process she goes through when writing a major feature article. She first sketches out the questions she wants to explore and does her research. Once she's got plenty of material she starts to write. But at this point she sometimes hits a crisis of confidence. Can she really write this piece? At the beginning of writing it can feel impossible. But she's been here before. She calls it the 'phase of disbelief'. It is temporary.

When she sticks with it, something clears and the words start to flow. The feature gets written.

One of the big shifts in finding power is to recognize the difference between being on the inside of a process and the outside. You're on the inside when you're taking the steps that move you towards your goal. You're on the outside when you've either not started or you've given up.

The way through disbelief is to stay inside, to trust that when you stick with the process of taking those steps, a path reveals itself. It can take a while for this to happen. But if you recognize that disbelief can be a phase you pass through, you're more likely to trust the process enough to stay inside it. Something else that can help you stay inside is to take regular renewal breaks.

The importance of pauses

The crop rotations of organic gardening include a fallow period where the soil is left to regenerate. Humans need fallow periods too. When you see rests and pauses as part of a larger process, you don't need to feel guilty when you take them. They are part of being productive. In sports training, peak performance is reached through alternating periods of activity with pauses for renewal. It is the same in our lives too. Many people find that they tend to have their most creative ideas during unhurried moments of rest. With the right balance of activity and relaxation, the pauses allow space for insight and inspiration to bubble up from the back of your mind.

> **Try this: Giving attention to the pause**
> Over the next seven days, pay special attention to the times when you stop. Notice how often you take breaks and whether you feel recharged by them. Explore different ways of using your pauses, so that they support the renewal and maintenance of your personal energy.

Crisis as turning point

One of the most useful aspects of process thinking is the way it can help us to think about crises. In my work in the addictions field, I notice that people often start to get most interested in change after things have gone badly wrong for them. Following a crisis or disaster, an addict may feel so awful that they think to themselves: 'I've had enough of this, I'm going to do something about it.' This can become the turning point referred to as hitting rock bottom.

One of my clients recently described this to me: 'I remember the day I started getting serious about my recovery. It was when I woke up in intensive care after a failed overdose.' She was so shocked to find herself there that she broke through the denial that had previously claimed her drinking wasn't much of a problem.

Turning points are not automatic. While in Chapter 8 we look in more depth at how you can turn a crisis into a turning point, process thinking provides the foundation for this. As well as acting as an antidote to the static thinking that says 'things will never get better', it also counters another type of thinking that can block personal power – all-or-nothing thinking.

Moving away from all-or-nothing thinking

Someone I knew described how she had always wanted to play the flute. She told me: 'I want to play like James Galway. Unless I'll be able to play like that there's no point in me even starting.' All-or-nothing thinking like this makes it very difficult to take the first steps of any change. Whenever you take up anything new, you start from the place of being a beginner. If it's an instrument, you don't sound too good. If it's a skill, you begin by not having it. Babies don't just get up and walk, they go through a long process of repeated failed attempts followed by trying again.

What process thinking offers is a way of looking at the current situation in the context of a wider time frame. When you can see yourself as part of a process that moves in the direction you want to go, it is easier to take the next step. The following exercise is a tool that I often use with people when they are feeling stuck, when they just can't see how to move forward. It is also useful any time you want to give your confidence a boost or identify your next step. Try it out and see where it takes you.

The scaling questions process
STAGE 1: IDENTIFY YOUR TARGET
Choose a goal or ambition that you want to move towards. (This exercise follows on well from the intentioning process on p 65.)

STAGE 2: SCALING QUESTIONS
Imagine (or even better draw on some paper) a line marked with a scale from 0 to 10. Ten out of ten represents reaching your dream, while zero marks

the point of complete absence of any progress at all. Sometimes people prefer to draw the line as a hill or mountain, where ten is reaching the top. While moving towards the dream can feel like an uphill climb, you can at least mark your progress along the way.

Where, on that 0–10 scale, would you put yourself at the moment? (See Figure 4.8.)

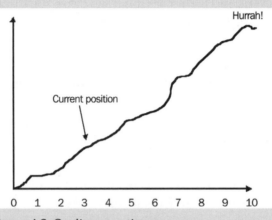

Figure 4.8 Scaling questions process

STAGE 3: OWNING YOUR STRENGTHS
If you have given yourself any points at all above zero, ask yourself what progress you've already made that has helped you to get this far. One way of owning your strengths and resources is to notice and name them. This is particularly important if your confidence is low, as it shifts attention onto the progress you have made and the steps you have already taken.

STAGE 4: NEXT STEP TARGET
If you were to identify a step towards your goal that you could confidently achieve in the next seven

> days, what would that be? It doesn't matter how
> small it is (for example it might only move you from
> 3 to 3.1).
>   Take that step and then identify another one.

The way we think about goals

One of my clients once told me about the time he got 98 per cent in a school physics exam. When he got home, his father asked: 'What happened to the other 2 per cent?' The father's response turned a great success into a failure.

Although this is an extreme example of all-or-nothing thinking, it illustrates how our experience of success is related to the way we look at things. In order to maintain motivation and determination, we need to believe that the steps we take are worthwhile. But if we feel that we are never reaching our target, it can be easy to lose heart. The way we think about our goals therefore makes a big difference to how achievable we believe them to be.

Three ways of thinking about change

Static thinking	You can't change things, they've always been like this. there's no point even trying.
All-or-nothing thinking	Unless you can change the whole lot or get all the way there, there's no point even starting.
Process thinking	Where do I want to get to? How far have I come already? What's the next step?

Process goals boost confidence

When taking up a musical instrument or learning a new skill, the main motivation may well be an attraction to the ideal of being able to do it. This is having a focus on the destination you want to reach, or on what we can call *outcome* goals. But there will be lots of smaller steps on the way to reaching that outcome. For example, if you want to learn to play the piano, you first need to gain access to a piano and then perhaps to arrange lessons. These are examples of what we can call *process* goals. Shifting your focus from outcome goals to process goals is a way to turn the feeling of failure into one of success.

When you first start the journey towards an ambitious goal, your desired outcome can seem impossibly far away. Even after lots of effort, when you look at the distance you've still got to go, it is easy to feel you're getting nowhere. If you only measure your progress by how far you've still got to travel, you can find yourself in a vicious cycle that drains confidence (see Figure 4.9).

Figure 4.9 A loop that drains confidence

You can turn this vicious cycle around by using the scaling questions exercise on p 90. This helps you identify process goals on the way to where you want to get to. By aiming for things you are likely to achieve, you set yourself up for success in a way that creates a self-amplifying loop that boosts confidence (see Figure 4.10).

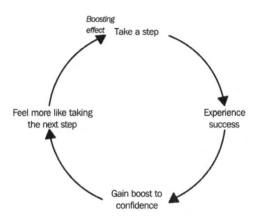

Figure 4.10 A loop that boosts confidence

I did the scaling questions exercise with a client who desperately wanted to find a partner. He had been single for many years and when he focused on the outcome goal of finding a girlfriend, his heart sank. He felt both powerless and hopeless. But when he focused on process goals, he recognized he had already made some progress, as having given up drinking made him a more attractive potential partner. He saw there were other steps he could take too, such as redecorating his home and learning to communicate better. What you're doing with process goals is identifying the practical action steps that move you closer to your goal. Often these have value in themselves, such that even if you never reach your final goal, the steps you've taken may still vastly improve your situation.

Cultural shifts

The focus of this chapter so far has been on individual change towards personal goals. However, the principles we've been exploring can be applied equally well to change at the level of groups, organizations and society. When looking at how to transform larger systems, static thinking is so common that many people believe you can't change the world. This belief is one way of looking at things; process thinking offers a different perspective.

If we see the present as just one frame in a larger unfolding process, it becomes easier to see how changes that seem impossible at one point in time can become possible in another. Events like Nelson Mandela becoming president in South Africa or the collapse of the Berlin Wall might have seemed unthinkable even a few years before they occurred. Further back in time, women campaigned for and got the vote in most countries; slavery was abolished in large parts of the world. These changes didn't just happen by themselves. They occurred because people took steps, did things, made choices. Lots of tiny actions added together to create larger cultural shifts and political transitions. In the same way, everything we do combines to create the history of tomorrow.

When addressing big issues like global warming or mass poverty, our actions can seem so insignificant that it is easy to believe they make no difference. This is particularly likely if we only focus on the outcome goal of solving the problem (see Figure 4.9). Focusing on process goals is a way of restoring the confidence that our actions are worthwhile. If we have concerns about big issues, we can become part of the process of responding to them. Our choices and actions are like the tiny movements from frame to frame and it is through these that bigger changes occur. Taking this perspective makes it easier to trust the process of larger change that can happen through us.

From optimism to breakthrough

The process thinking approach of this chapter is a key element in developing an optimistic thinking style. Research[1] shows that learned optimism reduces the risk of depression, can improve performance at work and can also lead to better physical health. While process thinking helps you develop optimism and confidence, what strengthens positive belief even more is when you have the experience of a breakthrough. Seeing really is believing. When you see yourself doing things that you'd previously thought of as beyond you, you finally cast off your old limiting beliefs like poorly fitting clothes.

However, to succeed in breaking through to this new level of personal power, you need the help of a more advanced toolkit. The focus of the next section is on how you find ways through blocks. It will offer you a set of principles and practices that can be used when facing any kind of obstacle. The first part of this is to find the courage even to attempt to tread into new ground. The next chapter shows how you can find this.

Power Points

1 If you view your personality, human nature or the world as essentially fixed and unchanging, it is difficult to develop the confidence that you can change things. This static thinking approach is a block to finding your power.

2 Process thinking views life as more like the constantly changing frames of a movie film, where if something isn't already in the picture it doesn't mean it never will be. Your choices and actions, like the tiny movements from one frame to the next, add together to make bigger changes happen.

3 Confusion, crisis and disbelief may all be stages in a larger process of change. Recognizing this helps you trust the process and keep going through difficult times.

4 Outcome goals identify the destination you want to get to, process goals identify the steps needed to get there. Focusing on process goals allows you to experience success in each moment even though you may still be far away from your destination. This helps maintain your optimism and determination.

5 The scaling questions process is a practical tool for identifying process goals. It also helps you recognize the distance you have already covered. This is important for maintaining motivation and confidence.

6 The way to trust a process is to find a way of playing a part in it. So long as you keep following the thread and taking the steps, then you remain on the inside of the process in a way that moves it forward.

Part II

*The Power to Move
Through Blocks*

*"Problems call forth our courage and wisdom;
indeed, they create our courage and our wisdom."*
M Scott Peck

5

How to Find Courage

*L*izzie was blocked by fear. Whenever she had to do anything in front of other people, she had a mini panic attack. 'I was so terrified of making a fool of myself that I just kept quiet or turned opportunities down,' she told me. Lizzie sometimes dreamt of being able to go on stage and perform, but such fantasies soon got shot down inside her mind. 'I was always questioning my ability and comparing myself with others,' she said. 'My fear of appearing stupid stopped me from trying anything new.' Because it felt safer to stay with what was comfortable and familiar, Lizzie became stuck in a comfort trap. To get out, she needed to find a way through her fear.

In this chapter, we look at how you find courage, introducing principles and practices for unlocking this essential ingredient of personal power.

Understanding the comfort trap

Significant change, even when it is attractive on the surface, tends to arouse fear. When you tread into unknown territory, this natural reaction protects you by increasing your alertness to potential threats. Fear also generates resistance to directions that your mind associates with danger, discouraging you from stepping beyond the ground you think of as safe.

While emotions like fear and anxiety can play an essential survival role, when they lead to overprotection problems arise. Being ruled by fear can make it difficult to move beyond the comfortable and familiar. This is the comfort trap. Once you recognize this, it becomes easier to see how the way out of the trap is through resistance. Facing fears is a normal and necessary part of stepping into new ground.

Each comfort trap has two main parts: a comfort zone and an edge. A good example of this is in agoraphobia, where there is an abnormal fear of public places. Agoraphobics tend to feel anxious when they leave the security of a familiar environment. Home is the comfort zone, but when stepping outside they cross a point (their edge) beyond which they start to feel nervous. For some that edge may be the end of their street, for others it might be the front door. Crossing this edge can be so frightening that some agoraphobics become prisoners inside their own homes.

Although severe agoraphobia is rare, the psychological processes that lie behind it are common. We are all likely to have areas of our life where we feel at home, as well as edges beyond which we start to feel uncomfortable (see Figure 5.1). We're happy with some types of change because they don't take us outside our comfort zone. But if a change risks moving us into areas where we feel less confident, then our mind may start telling us reasons for this not being such a good idea. Whenever you experience inner resistance like this, you can tell you've come up against an edge.

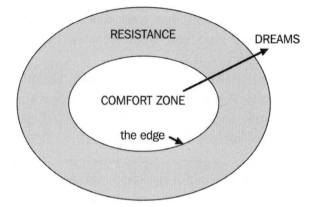

Figure 5.1 Dreams are often the other side of the edge

When you come to an edge, resistance can express itself in different ways. You may feel the intensity of fear, noticing your heart pounding or second thoughts racing through your mind. But resistance can also appear as cynicism, disbelief or lack of energy. If you feel sleepy as soon as you start an activity or area of conversation, consider the possibility that this could be resistance rather than tiredness or boredom.

There will be times when fear is based on good reasons so, whenever you come up against an edge, ask yourself what you might be wanting to protect yourself from. For example, I am in my comfort zone when I'm walking on the pavement. I see a very physical edge as I approach the road. I have a resistance to walking on the road based on an appropriate fear of getting hit by a car.

But what if the dream I want to head towards is over the other side of the road? I am then confronted with a choice: keep safe and give up my dream, or face fear and cross the road. In this case it is easy to see what the dangers are. But in many situations potential threats aren't as visible as approaching traffic. So instead, we use our imagination to consider what might lurk round the corner in time. When a dream pops up in our mind, a host of 'what ifs' often follow: 'What if I fail?' 'What if people think I'm stupid?' 'What if it does work out but it isn't as good as I hope?' The dream can get knocked down inside us before it has had a chance to take form. This is what happened to Lizzie who, as a result, often ended up feeling 'disappointed but safe'.

Threshold guardians

In his study of folk tales from around world, mythologist Joseph Campbell[1] identified stages that good stories tend to move through. After the call to adventure, it is common for the central characters to have second thoughts about setting off on their quest. There is usually some major obstacle blocking their path, and in the story structure he identified, Campbell referred to these as 'threshold guardians'. There might be a giant troll guarding a bridge or a haunted forest to travel through. If these obstacles always succeeded in blocking the way, the story would never go anywhere.

In the first Harry Potter book,[2] the call to adventure comes as the letter inviting Harry to study at the wizards' school Hogwarts. But Uncle Vernon disapproves and so tries to stop the letter getting through. He is a threshold guardian. Can you imagine how the story would have gone if he had succeeded?

Chapter 1   Call to adventure
Chapter 2   Obstacle in the way
Chapter 3   Main character can't see an easy or comfortable way through, so gives up
End of story

This is the comfort trap. The way out is to see obstacles not as dead ends that block the dream but as challenges to be faced.

Dealing with dreamblockers

All the 'what ifs' can be seen as threshold guardians that test your commitment, courage and ingenuity. Facing them becomes part of the adventure of finding your power. Fear, embarrassment, cynicism and disbelief can all be thought of as characters on your journey that patrol the points where you might cross into new ground. I call them dreamblockers because, if you let them, that is exactly what they will be. For the story you are part of to continue beyond the thresholds they guard, you need to find a way through.

This is where strategies for dealing with resistance and fear are needed. Here are seven:

◆ *Recognize your resistance.*
◆ *Remember your call to adventure.*
◆ *Challenge your objections.*
◆ *Identify small steps and take them.*
◆ *Prepare yourself.*
◆ *Find allies.*
◆ *Feel the fear and do it anyway.*

Recognize your resistance
A great deal of behaviour is governed by what psychologists call 'semi-automatic routines'. When you're walking you don't have to think about each step; when you're eating, you put food in your mouth even if you're thinking about something else. Such movements are under

conscious control when we want them to be, but if we've got other things on our mind, we can let the automatic part of our brain take over. This ability to automate aspects of our behaviour is remarkably useful. It frees the conscious brain from having to fuss over every detail in life.

Putting ourselves on auto-pilot like this allows us to perform complex tasks like driving a car, while at the same time having a conversation or planning the day ahead. But semi-automatic routines can also include avoidance reactions to anything we associate with fear. Without being aware of it, we may subconsciously turn away from people, places or topics of conversation that trigger anxiety.

The first time I went to an assertiveness class, I was asked to do a role-play that involved saying 'No' to a request. It seemed a simple task and as I batted off various requests, I felt I was doing well. But I was surprised to hear afterwards that I hadn't used the N-word once. My habitual avoidance of conflict was so deeply ingrained that I hadn't even noticed my resistance.

The first stage in dealing with any obstacle is simply to recognize it. If it remains unseen, it becomes an invisible barrier confining you to a comfort zone you may not even be aware of. If you ever suspect you might be sabotaging yourself from moving in a particular direction, pay special attention to what happens when you encounter opportunities to move that way. Be on the lookout for seemingly innocent decisions that block the progress you want.

> **Try this: Recognizing resistance**
>
> *If you experience frustration or disappointment in moving towards a goal, ask yourself these questions:*
> - *Is anything more important to me right now than reaching this goal?*
> - *What do I protect myself from by failing?*
> - *If I wanted to sabotage myself, how could I do that?*

Once you recognize a resistance, you can begin to explore what function it may be attempting to serve. My avoidance of the word 'No' protected me from confrontations, but I paid a high price. I ended up overloaded and unable to meet some of the expectations I generated. There were times when I let people down because I'd taken on more than I could deliver. My fear avoidance was a short-term fix that, in the long term, amplified the very problems I was trying to prevent.

Resistance occurs when there is a conflict between parts of you that want different things. Both parts may be expressing a need or value that is important to you, but while the resistance is subconscious, you're not in a position to choose or work out a way to satisfy both needs.

In my addictions work, I often see clients who tell me they want to stop drinking, but who show resistance by missing sessions. I think of this as a double signal, in that I'm getting two different messages from them. In their words they're telling me they want to change, in their actions they're communicating that they're not so sure. When we start exploring what might be scary or difficult about change, the resistance is brought into the open where it can be looked at and dealt with. Attendance at sessions often dramatically improves when we do this. But it still leaves the question: how can we face fears once they've been exposed?

Remember your call to adventure

With resistance, there are two different calls happening at the same time. The first is the call of your resolve to step forward, the second the call of all those parts of you that want to retreat. Your doubts and fears can be very persuasive. To find the determination required to face and move through them, you have to have good reasons. This is where you need to remember your call to adventure.

If fear is a threshold guardian blocking your path, why do you want to find a way through? What possible benefits are there for you? When you start collecting compelling motives, you motivate yourself. Three areas worth looking at are:

◆ *The positive consequences of moving forward.*
◆ *Any past memories of fears successfully challenged.*
◆ *The negative consequences of remaining blocked.*

If you did find a way through your resistance, what would be the best thing that could happen for you? When you start to think about this, notice how you feel. If this call to adventure is strong, you're likely to start feeling excited. Focusing attention on what you'd most like to happen is a way of building up enthusiasm for the journey ahead. To voluntarily wade through the swamps of discomfort and frustration, you need a vision so attractive that you think it's worth the effort.

When you make a decision to proceed in spite of the known risks, something interesting happens. Adrenalin pumps, your heart thumps and your skin may be moistened by sweat. You can feel more intensely alive. Facing fear is so thrilling that some people do it as a sport. The attraction behind bungee jumping is that there are two sides to fear: one is terror, the other is excitement.

You can boost your resolve by remembering times when you've successfully moved through initial reluctance to act. What past victories can you recall? Even the small ones are significant. Identify times when you've defied anxiety, acted anyway and had a positive experience as a result.

When you do this, you map out the sequence that defines adventures. First you notice a need that calls you and starts a journey towards a goal. Then you become aware of obstacles in the way. You may have second thoughts, but if your call is strong enough you're not put off. Seeing the block as a threshold guardian, you stretch your strength and ingenuity to find a way through. When you do, you're delighted. When you fail, you learn things that prepare you for your next attempt. What I'm describing here is the process thinking approach – you recognize that facing fear is a necessary part of the process by which both happiness and confidence grow.

When you're facing a choice of whether or not to do something, it is easy to get stalled by focusing on what can go wrong if you proceed. But what might happen if you don't move forward? Looking at the downside of staying where you are can generate the inspirational dissatisfaction needed to prompt change. A scary fear of any journey is that you might die on the way. But you can also die a little every day if you avoid the adventures you're here to live.

Challenge your objections
When you're aware of both your call to do something and
your resistance to it, how do you find courage to rise to
the occasion facing you? A proven strategy here is learning to challenge your objections. Fears are usually based
on a pessimistic assessment of what would happen.
Psychologist Martin Seligman[3] has this suggestion:

> *The key to disputing your own pessimistic thoughts is
> to first recognize them and then to treat them as if they
> were uttered by an external person, a rival whose mis-
> sion in life was to make you miserable.*

If someone falsely accused you of something, you might
rise to the occasion by defending yourself, telling your
attacker where they had got it wrong. But when we are
attacked or undermined by aspects of our own thinking,
we may be less used to standing up for (and to)
ourselves.

Rather than just having one personality, we can think
of our minds as being composed of a number of different
inner characters. The 'fearful self' is the part that always
worries about what might happen. The 'inner cynic' is the
part that offers a running commentary on why each new
plan is doomed to failure. While these unwilling aspects
of ourselves may protect us from wild goose chases, they
can also block initiative and personal power. If we are to
break through the negativity that keeps us trapped, learning ways to challenge them is essential.

How do you know whether negative thoughts are
based on appropriate cautions or exaggerated risk? The
way to find out is to challenge your inner cynic or fearful
self to be specific about their concerns, and then to

examine them. You listen to what they have to say and then give this a reality check. Here is a way of doing this.

Try this: Challenging your objections

When you notice fearful thoughts or inner cynicism, ask yourself whether this is an accurate assessment of the situation or an overly negative view. A useful way to tell the difference is to challenge the thought by first writing it down and then checking it against the following questions:

◆ *What is the evidence for and against this view?*

◆ *What is the effect of thinking this way?*

◆ *What other ways are there to look at this situation?*

◆ *Is the negative thought helping me or blocking my way?*

If the negative thought appears to be obstructive, replace it with a more encouraging view. Act on the positive statement. It will open up a new way forward.

Cognitive therapy has been shown to be an effective treatment for anxiety and depression.[4] It involves challenging negative thinking like this. Learning to argue back against your own cynicism and fear becomes a way of finding a more confident voice within yourself. This puts you in a stronger position to use the next strategy.

Identify small steps and take them

In the treatment of phobias, people are presented with the situations they find scary. They start at the easy end and work up from there. For example, if someone is terrified of spiders, the first step is to identify a scenario they feel comfortable with. This might just be being in the same room as a plastic spider. They then map out a series of stages between the least and the most scary, approaching the facing of their fear in manageable chunks. The principle here is that things become less scary once you get used to them and by taking steps you know you can cope with, you build up confidence. This is called progressive desensitization.

When you're facing fears in your own life, you can use the same approach. If you have a particular goal, like being able to speak in public, list a range of situations that involve expressing yourself. Then rank them in order of scariness. Aim for the step you feel most confident of taking. Do this a few times and when you feel comfortable doing it, move on to the next step. Like sports training, you start from where you are and aim for goals that stretch you a bit, but that you can also realistically achieve. With each mini-victory your confidence grows. But if you find yourself stretched too far, take a step back and get familiar again with doing well at the previous level (see Figure 5.2).

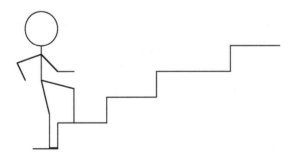

Figure 5.2 A step-wise approach to facing fear

Prepare yourself
Whenever you come to a step you're not ready to take, you can use the structure of the dream cycle to prepare yourself. First review the progress you've already made.

The mere fact that you are thinking about challenging your fears is a step in itself. Then identify what you'd like to happen. What is your ideal outcome? The planning stage involves looking at how you can move towards that.

An important part of this is doing background research, finding out more about the challenge you face so that you are better prepared to take it on. This is where it helps to deepen your understanding of fear and the range of factors influencing it.

Did you realize that anxiety tends to be more pronounced on an empty stomach? When blood sugar gets low your body's emergency response is triggered, which results in a release of adrenalin and increased nervousness. You can see the effects of this in young children when they get irritable before meals. Adults too are more sensitive to pressure when their blood sugar is low. You increase your ability to face stressful situations simply by ensuring that you don't go more than four waking hours at a time without having something to eat.

There is growing evidence that some diets make people more likely to have mood swings, while others promote emotional and physical wellbeing. For example, a research study[5] in a young offenders' unit showed a marked reduction in violent incidents among those taking a daily nutritional supplement of vitamins, minerals and essential fatty acids. A healthy diet can help you remain calm and centred when dealing with stress.

Diet is just one of a number of background factors that influence your reaction to fear. Also significant are physical exercise, adequate sleep, use of relaxation exercises, recovery time after stress, spiritual beliefs and avoiding alcohol and tobacco (as both these drugs increase long-term anxiety). By paying attention to background factors, you create a context that supports your courage.

Another useful preparation strategy is mental rehearsal. Each time you picture yourself successfully dealing with a scary situation, you strengthen your confidence that you can do it. A variant of this approach is used in the treatment of nightmares. First the person thinks of a way that the nightmare could have a good ending. Then, in a waking state, they imagine themselves back in the dream and picture the good ending happening. By building a successful turnaround into the story, they take the sting out of the nightmare's tail. Since fear is based on anticipation of a negative outcome, building in the possibility of a good ending can take much of the dread away.

Find allies

Among the most important background factors in facing fear is the support we get from others. Research has shown that when people face a challenging situation alone, they show higher levels of fear.[6] Just having someone they feel support from in the same room leads to measurable reductions in bodily measures of anxiety. If there is any situation you find too scary to face alone, take someone with you. When facing fear, the motto 'I can't, *we* can' points to one of our most enduring sources of courage.

In his book *The Art of Loving*, psychoanalyst Erich Fromm[7] states: 'The experience of separateness arouses anxiety; it is, indeed, the source of all anxiety.' When we feel a connection with a significant other, this can be a source of strength. I don't just mean people here. Pets, plants and symbols of spiritual significance can all be seen as allies. One of the people I interviewed told me: 'When

I need help, I think of my dad. Even though he died years ago, I know he's there, helping me.'

> **Try this: Identifying sources of strength**
> ◆ *Who or what do you turn to in times of need?*
> ◆ *Where are the sources of strength that lie beyond yourself?*

Feel the fear and do it anyway[8]

One evening eight years ago, Lizzie's life began to change. She went to a performance of Japanese taiko drumming. She found it completely exhilarating, loving the sound, the discipline, the physicality of it. In the back of her mind a fantasy sprouted. 'Maybe I could do that,' she wondered. But it seemed ridiculous. The next morning she returned to the usual busy-ness of her life as a painter and decorator.

Later that week, a friend mentioned that there was going to be a taiko drumming workshop at the weekend. 'Wow!' Lizzie thought. 'But I couldn't possibly go to something like that by myself.' She phoned around her friends, pleading with them to accompany her. One by one they made their excuses. Then finally someone said he'd go. But the evening before it was due to happen, he phoned to back out. Lizzie hardly slept that night. She was desperate to attend the workshop, but the thought of going by herself was just too scary to consider.

Lizzie recognized that she was at a choice point. She could remain blocked by fear and stuck in a comfort trap, or she could try something different. Lizzie decided to see the drumming workshop as a personal challenge. She remembered a friend telling her about a useful strategy when making a decision: imagine that you've made it one way and then ask yourself how you feel. Is it regret, relief or excitement? It may be a mixture of these, but if there is more disappointment than relief, then it is worth looking at your decision again. She knew how she'd feel if she didn't go to the workshop: disappointed but safe. This was familiar to her and this time she wanted something different. She decided to go.

She hadn't booked, she just turned up. She told herself that if she didn't like the workshop, she could always leave. The participants were asked one by one to go up to the taiko drum and make a big noise. 'You can't be mouse like around these instruments,' said Lizzie. 'They require a willingness to move beyond fears of being heard. I learnt something important that day. I learnt that it is OK to feel stupid in front of other people, because you get over barriers by doing that.'

By facing her embarrassment and surviving, Lizzie crossed the line out of her comfort trap. When I asked her what else she had learnt about facing fears, she said:

Life presents you with opportunities but it is up to you whether you take them. If you can't face a big challenge, then try something little. If it is just reachable, you're more likely to do it. But at some point, if you want to experience something new, you have to take the plunge.

In this statement, Lizzie is presenting two of the main principles used in the psychological treatment of fear and anxiety. In order to move beyond fears, at some point you need to face them. But that is much easier if you take small steps at a time and aim for what is just reachable.

Lizzie, like most people, still has fears that she finds difficult to face. But the evidence that this approach works for her has been the remarkable change in her life over the last eight years. Taking things little step by little step, Liz Walters has become one of the leading taiko drummers in the UK, and now performs and teaches internationally.

Power Points

1 Facing fear and resistance is a normal and necessary part of stepping into new ground. To do this, you need courage.

2 Seven strategies for finding courage are:

◆ **Recognize your resistance**: fears can act subconsciously, leading you to block or avoid opportunities without even being aware of it. The first stage in dealing with resistance is to recognize it.

◆ **Remember your call to adventure**: the courage to face fear grows out of having good reasons to do this. When you can see why it is worth the effort to push through resistance, this fuels your determination to keep going.

◆ **Challenge your objections**: fear is often based on an overly pessimistic assessment of risk. By learning to identify and challenge anxious thoughts, you develop a more confident voice within yourself.

◆ **Identify small steps and take them**: fear is best faced in manageable chunks. Things become less scary once you get used to them, and by taking steps you know you can cope with, you build up confidence.

◆ **Prepare yourself**: you put yourself in a stronger position to face challenging situations by training yourself and attending to background factors, such as diet, sleep and exercise, which influence your performance.

◆ **Find allies**: when you feel support around you, it strengthens you.

◆ **Feel the fear and do it anyway**: if you want to find a way through fear, at some point you have to face it. Say the magic words 'What the heck' and take the plunge.

6

How to Have Breakthroughs

*I*n one of the *Star Wars* films, Luke Skywalker sets out to reach the Jedi Master Yoda, but ends up crashing into a swamp. Yoda uses the power of 'the force' to raise Luke's spacecraft from the water. Looking on in amazement, Luke utters the words 'I don't believe it', to which Yoda replies, 'That is why you fail.'

When facing difficult challenges, you may often encounter the disbelieving voice that says: 'It can't be done.' Sometimes this might be right. But our view of what's possible is much influenced by the angle we look from. What's impossible with one way of looking may not be with another. A simple shift in perspective can open up new ways of moving forward.

This chapter introduces a set of creative problem-solving tools designed to help you find novel ways through obstacles. If you're ever feeling stuck and unsure about how to proceed, these tools could help you find the way to a breakthrough.

The first step is to challenge your disbelief

Until 1954, it was widely believed that a mile could not be run in less than four minutes; possible for gazelles perhaps, but not for human beings. Roger Bannister, a young medical student in London, didn't believe this. He set out to challenge the accepted view. He'd noticed that with regular training his times improved. He figured that if he continued this process and looked at ways of further enhancing his performance, he could eventually break the four-minute barrier.

Bannister didn't just train physically. He also trained psychologically. Practising mental rehearsal, he strengthened his belief that such a feat was possible by repeatedly running the race in his mind. When on the track, he enlisted the support of friends to run just ahead of him, helping him set the pace.

When we think about people who've succeeded in moving beyond previous limitations, it can help strengthen our belief that we too can do this. Stories like Bannister's are inspiring because they show that although something might appear impossible at one point in time, this doesn't mean it can't be done. In the year after Bannister ran his mile in less than four minutes, another 37 people managed to do the same. The next year, a further 300 runners did it too.

Try this: Challenging your disbelief

When you find yourself bumping into the belief that something is not possible for you, consider challenging this view.

You can do this by asking yourself the following three questions:

♦ *How do I know for certain that I can't do this?*
♦ *What other ways are there of looking at this?*
♦ *If there was a way of doing this, would I want to find it?*

As soon as you start questioning the certainty of your dis-belief, you invite the possibility that things might be different. Being too certain that something can't happen closes the door to finding a way.

The belief that something can't be done is only an assessment based on what you know at the time. As you learn new skills and acquire new information, that assessment can change. If you want to be completely realistic, the best way to do this is to keep an open mind. None of us can know for sure what might become possible in the future.

The second step is to develop frustration tolerance

When you defy disbelief and set out to accomplish something you'd previously assessed as beyond you, success might not come straight away. If so, you're likely to hit the next round of resistance: frustration. You get this feeling when you strongly want something to happen, but reality, for the time being at least, is working out differently.

Self-help writer Anthony Robbins[1] draws an important distinction here between frustration and disappointment:

> The message of frustration is an exciting signal. It means that your brain believes you could be doing better than you currently are. Frustration is very different from disappointment, which is the feeling that there's something you want in your life but you'll never get it.

Frustration is a signal that you've dared to step outside your comfort zone and take on a challenge that stretches you. The more difficult your challenge, the more likely you are to experience frustration. It is part of the territory. But the process thinking approach introduced in Chapter 4 can help make this easier to tolerate.

If you see frustration as one stage in a larger journey, it is viewed in a context that helps you recognize its positive side. Albert Einstein described genius as 1 per cent inspiration and 99 per cent perspiration. To accomplish something worthwhile often involves sweat. He also said: 'It's not that I'm so smart, it's just that I stay with problems longer.' To stay with a problem while a solution eludes you is frustrating. But if you can tolerate this, you won't be put off by difficulty. When you keep coming back to a challenging area and don't give up, you're more likely to find your way through to a breakthrough.

As we've already seen, outcome goals are the end result you'd like to happen, process goals are the steps taking you that way. By focusing on process goals, you can experience success even while the problem remains unsolved. What you're succeeding in is displaying the ability to continue in spite of frustration and difficulty. That takes determination, effort and courage.

The following exercise gives you an opportunity to experience this sort of success. I call it the three-minute frustration challenge. All you have to do is attempt the dots puzzle for at least three minutes. If you can manage longer, your benefits will be greater.

Try this: The three-minute frustration challenge
Your task is to join the nine dots shown below, using
no more than four straight lines, drawn without lift-
ing your pen off the paper or going backwards over
any line you have already drawn.

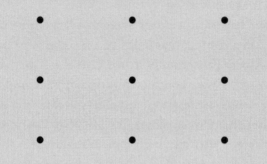

How did you get on? Did you try it? If you didn't, ask yourself what got in the way. The obstacles that stop us trying small things are often reflections of what gets in the way of bigger goals. Not having the confidence that it will be worth your effort, for example, is what often stops people taking that first step. But also to take any step you need a call to adventure. Would you do this puzzle if you were paid a large fee to do so? If you get the message behind this exercise, it could be worth more to you than money. It could change your life. But the way to this benefit is *through* the frustration. If you haven't already, I encourage you to give the exercise a try.

If you attempted the puzzle, congratulate yourself. The success lies in taking the step. If you experienced some frustration, that is even better. (If you didn't, it may be worth having another go and trying for longer.) If you solved the puzzle, that's a bonus. But if, like me, you found this extraordinarily difficult, you may be reassured to hear that it is unusual for people to solve it first time round.

When I first tried this puzzle, I struggled and struggled. I took breaks then came back to it several times, but I just couldn't see how to do it. What made this puzzle difficult for me was the way I was looking at it.

When I'm faced with a puzzle or challenging situation, I often focus in on the problem. This was the way I looked at the dots. Just as if I were using a zoom lens, my attention narrowed in to target the puzzle and exclude anything else that might be distracting. We do this whenever we focus our attention on something. It is as though our brain places a boundary or frame around what we're looking at, so that this becomes the foreground and everything else is background. The foreground is sharply in focus, the background may seem almost to disappear. This is our mind's way of concentrating its thinking power on a limited area.

For many types of puzzle and problem, this way of looking works really well. For example, when surgeons are operating they give their focused attention to the part of the body they're operating on. With surgical towels draped around the incision area, this may be the only part of the patient they see.

This frame of attention is based on our assumptions about what we consider worth looking at. When looking at the puzzle, I assumed that the dots were what I needed to focus on. Without consciously thinking about it, my mind drew a boundary around the problem, creating a box around the dots (see Figure 6.1). I assumed that the answer must lie in this space.

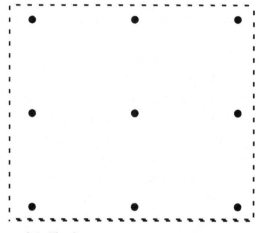

Figure 6.1 The box

When I ask participants on my courses to do this puzzle, they nearly all approach it this way. Like me, they end up being frustrated (see Figure 6.2).

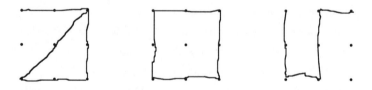

Figure 6.2 Attempted solutions

Whenever we look at anything, we always look *from* somewhere. We begin from a starting point of assumptions about where and how to look. What is important to focus on and what isn't? Where does the puzzle begin and where does it end? The way we frame any problem will determine how we tackle it. We look for answers within the frame created by our assumptions, and if we can't see a solution inside this space, we tend to assume that there isn't one.

The third step is to think outside the box

If the first step towards a breakthrough is to challenge your disbelief and the second is to develop frustration tolerance, the third is to think outside the box. This means thinking outside the frame of your usual assumptions, so that you look for different types of solutions. When you do this, you generate the sort of ideas that you would never normally have thought of.

How does this help with the dots puzzle? Figure 6.3 shows the first line of one possible solution.

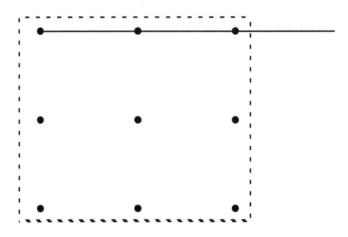

Figure 6.3 Thinking outside the box

And Figure 6.4 is one way in which the puzzle can be solved.

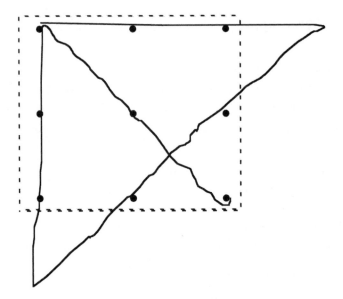

Figure 6.4 Some solutions move beyond limiting assumptions

Placing ourselves in a box

A friend told me she hadn't tried the puzzle because she knew it wasn't the sort of thing she was good at. All of us have weak areas where experience or other people have taught us that we're unlikely to succeed. Giving up before we start can be a way of avoiding frustration, embarrassment or disappointment. However, just as it is possible to create a limiting frame that restricts the way we look at puzzles, we can also do something similar when looking at ourselves.

Each of us has a self-concept that defines our sense of who we are and what we are capable of (see Figure 6.5). Some activities fall easily within the frame of what we see as possible for us, while others don't. For example, whenever we think 'I'm not the sort of person who does that kind of thing' or 'I can't see myself doing that', we're describing something that is outside the box for us.

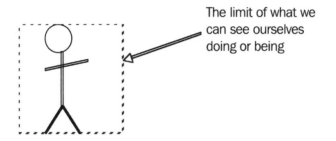

The limit of what we can see ourselves doing or being

Figure 6.5 We see our abilities within the frame of our self-concept

When Betty was 10 years old, she was told that she couldn't sing. When singing at school, a teacher told her it would be better if she just mouthed the words, so other people wouldn't have to hear her. So Betty grew up with the belief that she couldn't sing. It became part of her self-concept, and she assumed that this was just the way she was made. For decades she accepted this and avoided situations where she might have to sing.

In her 60s, she was feeling adventurous one summer and went to a voice workshop. I was there and shall never forget the look of pure joy on her face when Betty discovered that she could sing after all.

When we challenge limiting self-beliefs and step outside our usual way of doing things, the results can be liberating. You can do this by experimenting with different versions of yourself. If ever you find yourself blocked from moving in a particular direction, ask yourself if it would be easier if you were a different kind of person. As an experiment, imagine that you are. Try it out and see how it feels. It is possible to reinvent yourself.

> **Try this: Expanding possibility**
> ◆ *When you find yourself coming up against a block, think of someone you greatly admire.*
> ◆ *Imagine that, just for a moment, you have become that person. How would they respond to the situation you're in?*
> ◆ *Consider their response as an alternative option to what you would normally do.*

When you imagine yourself as someone else, you are stepping into a different state of possibility. You are placing yourself within an alternative frame of reference. If you imagine how several of your most admired people might respond to your current situation, you open up a range of perspectives and give yourself a wider choice of options.

Another approach is to imagine that you have become the very best possible version of yourself.

> **Try this: Ponder point**
> *Read the next sentence, then close your eyes and ponder.*
> ◆ *If you had as much courage, wisdom and determination as you would like, what could you do?*

Your imagination is a useful and practical tool, as it allows you to consider a wider range of possibilities. This can protect you against getting boxed into too small a frame of viewing things. Asking other people how they would respond also opens up options. This is different from asking for advice. You're not asking what they think you should do – you're asking what they would do in your situation. Sampling a wide range of perspectives helps you step outside the limits of your own view. The goal is to widen your range of options. It is up to you what you actually decide to do.

How do the suggestions in the previous few paragraphs sound to you? Are they things that you could see yourself doing? If you notice yourself having a dismissive reaction to something, it could be that it just isn't suitable for you. On the other hand, the ideas we are most dismissive of tend to be those that lie outside our box. This may be because they break one of our personal rules.

Boxed in by rules

As well as assumptions about where or how to look, we also make assumptions about how we should best respond to situations. These can become unwritten rules we place on ourselves, based on what our experience or culture has taught us is the proper way to act.

Personal rules serve an important function, helping us keep our behaviour within the bounds of what we believe will be acceptable and effective. Some of these rules are based on our own system of values, but others we may have picked up without really thinking about them.

Take the dots puzzle as an example. Years of childhood dot-to-dot puzzles had instilled in me certain beliefs about the proper way to do these things. In my mind I had an unwritten rule that lines should be drawn from one dot to another. It didn't occur to me that a line could go on past a dot and stop in mid-page (see Figure 6.6).

Figure 6.6 The line that broke the rule

Did you try to solve the puzzle by only drawing lines with dots at both ends? Often we aren't aware of rules like this, as they tend to occur at a level of thinking below conscious awareness. But the effect they can have is to limit us. If something can't be done in a particular way, we might easily assume it can't be done at all.

We know that an idea breaks a personal rule when it feels like the sort of thing we would never do. It might even seem outrageous, or somehow wrong. However, ideas that initially seem off the wall can sometimes lead to a breakthrough.

Doing the unthinkable

I recently spoke to a friend who was dissatisfied with her job. She told me: 'I know what I'd really like to do, but it's impossible.' What she most wanted was to cut her working hours so she could spend more time with her young daughter. She recognized she had become rather set in her ways, getting used to a level of spending that required her current income. When she realized how her assumption about money was blocking her, I saw a change in her eyes. She looked excited. It wasn't impossible to cut her hours down, but it would involve challenging her assumptions about how much money she needed. She had had a breakthrough.

Discoveries and breakthroughs usually share one thing in common: they move beyond a previously accepted assumption or convention. When you feel stuck, it is worth considering whether you're limiting yourself to a particular approach. You may not even be aware you've made a limiting assumption until you come across an approach that steps outside of it, so a useful tool here is lateral thinking.

Edward de Bono, the man who invented this term, wrote[2]:

> Lateral thinking is both an attitude of mind and also a number of defined methods. The attitude of mind involves a willingness to try to look at things in different ways. It involves an appreciation that any way of looking at things is only one amongst many possible ways.

Try this: Lateral thinking
Feeling blocked? See how many different ways you can think of to look at the issue you face. Write them down on a piece of paper. Aim to fill the page without stopping to judge.

Stepping-stone ideas

Generating a list of different ways of looking at something may not in itself solve a problem. But it takes you out of the view that there is only one way to look. It can be fun to think of wild and outrageous approaches and, when these break personal rules, it makes you more aware that you have those rules.

Some ideas can be called stepping-stone ideas. While they may not be realistic themselves, if they help you think in a different way then this might be a step towards finding an approach that does work.

For example, one of my frustrated, crazy attempts at solving the puzzle was to draw a messy squiggle over the dots. Looking at that helped me think of drawing one really thick line (for example with a giant marker pen) through all the dots, leading to another solution (Figure 6.7).

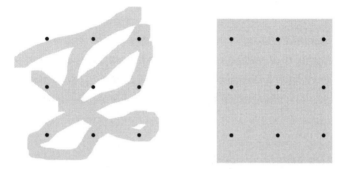

Figure 6.7 A stepping-stone idea

What we're looking at here is how we can open up a creative flow where previously there was a block. Strategies that help people think outside their usual approaches can be highly effective in turning around feelings of stuckness. Whenever you're not sure what your next step is or you're feeling short of inspiration, creative problem-solving strategies can be used to open up a way forward.

Here is my personal favourite. If you get familiar with using this technique, it could become a friend for life.

The five-stage problem-solving process

STAGE 1: CLEARLY DESCRIBE AND DEFINE THE PROBLEM
◆ Ask yourself: 'What's the problem I want to address?'

Write down your response. Sometimes more than one thing comes tumbling out. Let it roll, write whatever comes. But then look at what you've written and choose the main issue you want to tackle.

◆ *Ask yourself: 'Why is that a problem?' Write down your response.*

Repeat this process several times. What you're doing here is exploring exactly what it is you find difficult. Often problems have different layers and parts to them. A process like this can help you become more aware of what these are.

◆ *Choose the main aspect of the problem you want to tackle and write it down in the form of 'The problem is...' This becomes your working definition of the problem you are aiming to respond to.*

Example

John was an alcoholic man in his 50s who, for the last few nights, had been having problems sleeping. What was going through his head as he lay in bed were concerns about a family gathering at the weekend. He was dreading it and didn't want to go.

'Why is that a problem?' I asked him.

He told me he was worried his brother would be there.

'Why is that a problem?'

He hadn't spoken to his brother for over a decade as the last time they'd met they'd fallen out badly.

'Why is that a problem?'

He was worried they might have another row or, even worse, a fight. He didn't know how to handle the conflict with his brother.

While the problem initially seemed to be about sleep, asking 'Why is that a problem?' revealed what was happening under the surface. John decided that the thing he was most concerned about was the conflict with his brother, so his problem description became: 'The problem is that I have an old conflict with my brother and I don't know how to handle it if I see him at the weekend.'

> ### Stage 2: List possible responses
> When I do this in groups, I get a big blank piece of paper and suggest we completely fill this with possible responses, aiming to get at least 25 (and ideally more). If you are doing this by yourself don't be put off by big numbers. Start with three responses, then see if you can get up to ten. Anything over this just increases your choice.

At this stage you are only generating options and not judging their potential value. This embargo on judgement is important, as it separates the creative process from the editing, freeing you to be playful and experimental in your responses. You can do this process by yourself, but doing it with a friend can make it more fun and widen the range of options you generate.

Continuing with the example of John, here are the sort of responses that came up in the group.

1 Have a drink.
2 Leave the country.
3 Don't go to the family gathering.
4 Go with a friend.
5 Write to brother beforehand suggesting a 'cease-fire'.

6   Have counselling session with brother.
7   Avoid brother at gathering.
8   Write to apologize to brother.
9   Speak to other family members.
10 Join the Foreign Legion.
11 Arrange meeting with brother, show him you've changed.
12 Apologize to family in advance for not going.
13 Go for just a short while.
14 Give yourself permission to leave early if feeling need to exit.
15 Read self-help books about dealing with conflict.
16 Learn anger management strategies.
17 Organize own smaller family gathering at another time.
18 Explore own resentments to brother.
19 Try and understand brother's position.
20 Seek family therapy or mediation.
21 Hire a bodyguard.
22 Learn martial arts.
23 Put recovery first.
24 Arrange support afterwards, e.g. meet up with friend.
25 Accept that a decade-old conflict may not be sorted in a weekend, so develop longer-term plan for reconciliation. This may mean missing the family gathering.

When someone describes a problem they feel hopeless about, their energy often sinks. It isn't surprising then that the first few options on the list are exit strategies. John feels caught between a *must* and a *can't*. He feels he must go to the gathering, but he can't cope with the prospect of meeting his brother. Feeling cornered like this creates enormous psychological tension, explaining the sleepless nights. However, when you generate lots of response options, energy rises, as you break out of the feeling that there is no choice. You also move from an experience of defeat to one of success, as producing a list of 25 options, although initially daunting, is an easily achievable goal.

Some options appear extreme, but can serve a function in giving expression to bottled-up feelings. For example, 'hire a bodyguard' communicates a fear of physical threat. This is a stepping-stone idea that draws attention to issues of personal safety.

> *STAGE 3: DELETE OPTIONS THAT ARE UNACCEPTABLE TO YOU*
> *If there's any option you're not willing to consider, cross it out. Knowing you can do this makes it easier to be more adventurous at Stage 2. If an option is fine for someone else but isn't for you, put a line through it. Having the freedom to reject any response you don't want to consider can be liberating.*

John crossed out options 1, 2, 5, 6, 10, 11, 12, 17, 21 and 22.

> *STAGE 4: PICK OUT THE CHERRIES*
> *This is the stage to focus in on the options you're most interested in. I call these the cherries, as you are picking those you consider most tasty.*
> ◆ *Identify the ones you think most promising and mark them with a star.*
> ◆ *Weigh up the advantages and disadvantages of each of these and decide which ones you'd be willing to commit yourself to taking further.*

John liked the idea of looking at his own feelings of resentment towards his brother, because if he could find a way of working through some of these that would make him feel calmer. He also found option 25 reassuring. It recognized that there was an issue to face, but didn't put pressure on him to sort this out immediately. If he did go to the family gathering, he thought the most constructive option was to make sure he had the support of a friend.

STAGE 5: IDENTIFY ACHIEVABLE NEXT ACTION STEPS

What can you do in the next seven days? Identify at least one specific and realistically achievable step you can take.

Only list steps you can fairly confidently commit yourself to carrying out. Can you make a promise to yourself that you will do these? If so, you can reinforce your commitment by telling someone else and/or by writing your action steps down. For example:

My next action step is to ....
I will do this by (date) ....
Signed ....
I will also ....
I will do this by (date) ....
Signed ....

John agreed to phone a friend and ask if she would come to the family gathering with him. He also arranged to meet with his counsellor before the weekend to talk through some of the issues. And he agreed to give himself permission to back out of attending at the last minute if he felt that going would be too much for him. In the past, worries about a family gathering like this would have been a typical trigger for heavy drinking. But the process of generating a wide range of alternative responses helped John think outside the box of his usual responses, leading him to challenge his long-held view that he wouldn't be able to cope without a drink.

Thinking outside the box about power

The principles of creative problem solving can be applied to any area of life. The starting point is accepting that any way of looking is only one among many possible views. This is particularly true of the way we look at power.

If we assume that power is only based on things that we own, like money, status or even personal qualities, then it is easy to feel powerless without these. Power opens up when we identify different ways of thinking about it. For example, what if power was something that happened through you?

The word *through* has several meanings. We think of something as passing through when it comes in one end and goes out the other. Electricity, for example, involves a current of energy moving from a source to an output. When passing through a light bulb, the output is light; when through a radio, the output is sound. If you were to think of personal power in a similar way, then what could you plug into in order to power yourself up?

When I interviewed people about their sources of personal power, I noticed times when they became particularly alive. They sat up straighter, moving their hands as they spoke; they had energy in their voice and a brightness in their eyes. This happened when they were talking about the purposes that most inspired them. What's more, I often felt energized after these interviews. Something had been transmitted through them to me. Could inspiring purposes, I wondered, act as a form of personal electricity? To test out this theory, I'd like to share with you one of the stories I heard. See if it lights up your inner light bulb of inspiration.

After the Soweto rent strikes in the 1980s, the South African authorities stopped services to the township. With no rubbish collections, the waste started to pile up. Open spaces became dumping grounds.

Concerned by the deteriorating environment, Soweto resident Mandla Mentoor started an organization called Amandla Waste Creations. Amandla means power, and what Mandla did was use the power of creativity to turn rubbish into works of art. Enlisting community volunteers, some of them children, Mandla's project began to transform the local landscape. In 2001, he won an award of 10,000 Rand in recognition for his services.

Close to the neighbourhood where he lived was one of the main rubbish dumps of the township. A barren hill with an old water tower at the top, it was regarded as a dangerous place of foul smells and dead bodies, where people went to commit suicide. When Mandla looked at the hill, he had an inspiring idea. How would it be to restore this site and turn it into a symbol of hope?

Mandla used the money from his award to finance the clean-up operation. Initially volunteers needed protective clothing as the site was so contaminated. But slowly, the hill began to change. In less than a year, it had become an ecocultural resource centre where hundreds gathered for community events. When I interviewed Mandla in London in 2003, he told me about the learning centre at the top of this hill, where local people gather for dance, theatre, music and environmental projects. It is called SOMOHO, or Soweto Mountain of Hope.

The power of looking differently

Some situations can seem just as impossible as Luke Skywalker's when he crashed into the swamps: the mountain of Soweto rubbish faced by Mandla Mentoor; the four-minute mile; even the dots puzzle. Breakthroughs seem impossible before they happen because they break through a previously accepted view about what is achievable. What this means is that sometimes it is our view of reality, rather than reality itself, that stops us finding a way forward.

Power Points

1 If there's something you want to do, but you can't see how to do it, three steps to finding a breakthrough are:

- **Challenge your disbelief:** you can never know for sure that something is impossible. Be realistic by keeping an open mind and accepting that if you start looking for a way, you might find one.
- **Develop frustration tolerance:** frustration is a signal that you've stepped outside your comfort zone and taken on a challenge that stretches you. If you can tolerate this feeling, you won't be put off by difficulty.
- **Think outside the box:** step outside your usual way of looking. See how many different approaches you can think of. Stepping-stone ideas may seem crazy, but can lead to breakthroughs.

2 If you ever catch yourself thinking 'I'm not the sort of person who could do that', consider the possibility that this can change. Stretch your self-concept by challenging your old view of yourself.

3 The five-stage problem-solving process encourages lateral thinking, making it easier to step outside your usual approach:

◆ Identify the problem: 'The problem is...'
◆ Generate a list of possible responses.
◆ Delete responses you're not willing to consider.
◆ Pick out the cherries.
◆ Identify an achievable action step and commit to doing it.

4 Inspiring purposes can act through us, energizing us like a form of personal electricity. This is an example of power through.

7

Shifting Stuck Patterns

'Why does this keep happening to me?' cried Jenny in despair. She'd read self-help books, been on personal development seminars and attended therapy sessions. She had moved on in many ways. But every now and then she found herself falling back to a situation that was painfully familiar. Jenny nodded when I described this to her as the 'here I am again' point. 'That seems to be the story of my life,' she said. 'The question is, can I change it?'

Do you recognize this? Even when you've made great positive strides, there may still be days when you find yourself right back at the point you'd wanted to move on from. What I'm describing are stuck patterns. The next page gives some examples.

On the surface these might seem like three very different situations. But what they have in common is the unwelcome return of a painfully familiar experience. This chapter explores what makes some patterns of behaviour so resistant to change, while also introducing personal power strategies to help you make changes in the places you feel stuck.

- ◆ *Jim had been trying to control his anger, but last week he flipped again, had a major row and nearly lost his job.*
- ◆ *Although Paul had given up smoking, he gave in to temptation at a party. The next day he woke up hungry for nicotine. His addiction had returned.*
- ◆ *Tony and June are at it again. They've had this argument before, but it keeps replaying. They're both sick of it.*

What is a stuck pattern?

A pattern is anything that keeps repeating in a similar way. If you often have the same response to a particular situation, then this is one of your patterns. As your responses interact with those of other people, patterns occur in relationships, families, groups and organizations as well. A similar sequence of events can get played out again and again, even if the people occupying particular roles within it change. Recognizing these repeating patterns behind events can help you understand what's going on when you have that 'here I am again' feeling. When you get to know a pattern well enough, it also becomes easier to identify the points at which you can change it.

Not all patterns are bad. The reason you start repeating something is because, initially at least, it serves a function for you. The problem comes when you get so in the habit of doing things a particular way that you continue this even when it no longer helps. And if a pattern is deeply ingrained, you can find yourself doing it even when you've made a decision not to. These are the patterns that have got stuck.

The first stage in changing a pattern is simply to recognize it. Don't be put off if there's something you've
tried to change many times before but failed. The secret
of success in shifting stuck patterns is persistence coupled
with a few good tools. The first tool is awareness.

> **Try this: Identifying patterns I want to shift**
> Complete the following sentence, seeing what words
> naturally follow:
> ◆ 'Things I find myself doing even when I've
>   decided not to include...'
> An alternative is:
> ◆ 'Situations that happen too often for me
>   include...'
> Having identified some patterns, choose one that you
> would like to change.

Different ways of understanding what's going on

When something keeps happening and you'd prefer it
didn't, there are a number of ways of understanding what's
going on. The way you think about patterns will influence
your ability to change them. Here are four alternative
views.

It's just the way things are

There are some recurring themes that seem to be features
of life. We get sick from time to time, make mistakes,
upset other people. Having an attitude of acceptance can
make life easier to deal with. But how do you know
whether a pattern is an inherent feature of your life or a
temporary condition you might be able to change?

When I first met Jim he described himself as an angry person. He had a short fuse and would period- ically explode with rage. His father had been like this too and he wondered whether it might be genetic. When Jim saw his temper as part of the way he was, as a design fault, then he tended to think of it as something he couldn't change. To explore a different way forward, I asked him whether there were any exceptions, any occasions when he was provoked but didn't explode.

As Jim described difficult situations he'd dealt with calmly, he heard himself contradict the view that he was a hopelessly angry person. Exceptions show that something else is possible. He wasn't always angry, just sometimes. So what made the difference?

It's down to luck

The luck theory explains events in terms of chance hap- penings. If something difficult keeps happening, it is seen as bad luck. When it works out well for a change, it must be a lucky day. What's attractive about this approach is that there is no blame when things go wrong. But looking this way makes it less likely that you will look for the deeper causes behind events.

Initially Jim dismissed his occasional ability to handle things well as those being 'just good days'. But by becom- ing curious about what makes some days good and others bad, it becomes possible to identify trends and causal relationships.

Who or what is to blame?

While the last two perspectives promote a passive acceptance of repeated mishaps, the blame theory assumes that
someone or something is at fault. This is the approach
that demands an inquiry, seeking to assess evidence and
uncover what's really going on. The value of this is that it
sees repeating patterns as significant. If something keeps
happening, it is worth exploring what might be behind
this. There is a problem here though, and that is to do
with the way people often respond to blame.

When I was a child I used to play a game with my sib-
lings called 'It's not my fault'. On family journeys we'd sit
in the back of the car and after a while a squabble would
occur. When my parents turned around to tell us to stop,
each of us would announce in turn: 'It's not my fault, they
started it.' Like a hot potato that no one wanted to hold,
blame would get bounced around between us. Each of us
wanted to appear squeaky clean and so pointed the finger
of fault at someone else. In doing that, we closed our eyes
to any role we may have played in keeping the squabble
going. This blame game also gets played out in relationships, organizations and international politics. It can be a
potent blocker of personal power. Here's why.

Blame is based on a punishment model, where those
responsible for unwelcome events tend to be seen as bad
people who deserve to suffer. The shame associated with
being accused is uncomfortable. So it becomes the seat
that no one wants to sit on. Because blame threatens the
view that you are a good person, people may be unwilling
to look at or acknowledge their role when things go
wrong. Yet this defensiveness is precisely the opposite of
what's needed for personal power. To be able to change
something, you need to recognize ways in which you can

influence it. That means tracking down your role, even if it is a small one.

'We're going to find those responsible and make them pay.' Have you heard this phrase before? Does it encourage you to become more responsible? Blame cultures make it risky to take the lead or show initiative, because if things go wrong you'll be to blame. Whenever inaction is seen as a safer option, apathy is likely to be the dominant response. To find our power, we need a different way of thinking.

What's the pattern and how do I participate in it?
The questions 'Who's to blame?' and 'What's the pattern?' lead to different ways of seeing the same situation. Here's an example.

> *I saw a client with his wife for couple counselling. He was an alcoholic and always had a secret supply of alcohol in or near the house. His wife would search for this and pour it down the sink. He would become ever more crafty and find ingenious hiding places. The wife's view was that she searched because he hid. If only he wasn't so secretive, she wouldn't have to waste her time bottle hunting.*
>
> *The husband had a different view. He saw his hiding of drink as a logical response to her searching for it. If any alcohol were visible, she would pour it away. When he was desperate for a drink, he wanted to know that he had access to it. So he'd always keep an emergency supply hidden just in case.*

The question 'Who's to blame?' is likely to provoke an argument that is familiar to both of them. It goes like this:

she blames him, he blames her, she feels angry at being blamed, so does he, he goes off and drinks, she becomes more determined to hunt the booze, he becomes more convinced he needs it to cope with the arguments. Can you see how they've become locked into a pattern that reinforces itself?

Identifying patterns behind events provides a different way of thinking about cause and effect than the usual linear explanations. A linear explanation is in the form of *A* causes *B*. If we draw this as a diagram, the arrow goes one way like this.

A (cause) ⟶ B (effect)   Example: he hides ⟶ she searches

However, things are rarely as simple as this. Usually there are many causal influences happening at the same time. For example, the husband identified a cause-and-effect chain going the other way, like this.

B (cause) ⟶ A (effect)   Example: she searches ⟶ he hides

Bringing these two chains together creates a self-amplifying loop. Patterns get stuck when there is a causal loop like this keeping them going.

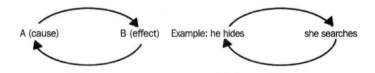

A (cause)   B (effect)   Example: he hides   she searches

This shift in thinking from lines to loops is key to understanding what makes some patterns so sticky. With an amplifying loop, a behaviour can cause itself to happen more. But if we recognize the role we play in one of these loops, we can change what we do and break the cycle.

When this couple saw how they both played a role in keeping their 'hide and seek' pattern going, they were able to reach an agreement to stop this. She gave up hunting for bottles, accepting that it was for her partner to make his own choices about his drinking. Reducing the conflict at home made it easier for him to stick to his decision to stop drinking.

When working with families of people with drinking problems, I need to tread a careful path if I am to help them identify their influence without leaving them feeling blamed. For example, it would be very unfair to suggest that the wife is the cause of her husband's behaviour. It isn't her fault that he has an alcohol problem. Notice the link between the last two sentences. If someone is seen as the cause, then the problem is regarded as their fault. It is worth looking closely at this way of thinking, as it goes to the heart of what makes it difficult to shift stuck patterns.

The old blame model assumes that fault lies in some people and not in others. Searching for the cause of a problem involves identifying the faulty people responsible for it. Judgements are then made about who is innocent or guilty, good or bad, sick or well.

The pattern view is based on a different way of thinking. For example, which square in Figure 7.1 overleaf is responsible for the circle?

Whenever you reduce a complex problem down to a single cause, you're in danger of missing out large parts of the story. This is because patterns are created by a number of influences acting together. Although some factors are bigger causes than others, each one, by itself, isn't enough to cause the whole problem.

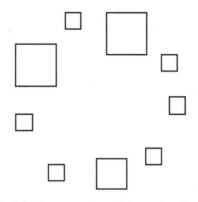

Figure 7.1 Which square is to blame for the circle?

What often happens is that while a debate rages about which of the larger influences is to blame, smaller causes get ignored. Whenever people say 'It's all down to…' or 'The root cause is…' they are identifying a single factor as the cause. But with stuck patterns, you can deal with what seems to be the primary cause and still find that the problem keeps coming back.

In the late 1980s I went through a period of clinical depression. It had reached the point where I was thinking about killing myself. Yet I was resistant to getting medical help because I blamed my mood disturbance on my working conditions. To go on antidepressants and continue crazy hours as a hospital doctor seemed like smashing a car's warning light when the oil level is low. Depression can sometimes be a warning signal telling you that your way of living is out of balance. I didn't want to see a psychiatrist if they might put it all down to a chemical imbalance in my brain. I chose the campaigning response instead.

I regarded my depression as an occupational injury, so I took my employers to court. If workers lose fingers in a sawmill because the machines lack safety precautions, the employers are seen as responsible. In a similar way, if a system of work pushes employees to dangerous levels of sleep deprivation, there needs to be a way of protecting safety. There wasn't. In the previous few years I'd worked shifts of over 104 hours and had weeks when I'd been on duty for more than 135 hours. With evidence linking sleep deprivation to both depression and mistakes at work, the system I worked under was unsafe. It felt clear to me that the cause of my depression was my job. However, while occupational stress was certainly a major factor, there was something this theory didn't explain.

Six months later I'd given up work, was sleeping well and didn't have much stress. I was no longer exhausted or suicidal, but I still felt depressed. I wondered what was causing this. I couldn't blame my job any more because I didn't have one.

I saw a psychotherapist to help me work out what was going on. I talked about my childhood, including some grizzly experiences like being sexually abused by a teacher at school. I also looked at what was happening in my life, the tensions between the different parts of me, the feelings that had been lurking under the surface. It was an unravelling process that definitely helped. But I also felt impatient with myself. Why was I still depressed? This question led me to a disturbing idea.

Was it possible that I was to blame for my depression? Could I be doing something that was keeping me depressed? Initially I reacted against this idea. It seemed like victim blaming. Not only did I feel low, but this view left me feeling guilty about it too. It suggested that I only had myself to blame because if I thought more positively then I'd be happier. What this perspective didn't appreciate was how difficult it is to think positively when you're low.

Looking back, I can see now that I was caught up in 'who's to blame' thinking. Blaming others freed me from guilt but left me feeling like a victim. The alternative of self-blame filled me with shame in a way that reinforced my low mood. To get well, I needed to recognize my role without feeling that the problem was all my fault.

What helped me here was a way of thinking about the difference between blame and responsibility. Blame looks back in time for someone to point the finger at; responsibility looks forward in time, asking: 'Which way do I want to go and how can I move in that direction?' Finding *response-ability* like this is at the core of what personal power is about.

There is also a difference between being responsible *for* something and responsible *towards* something. Being responsible for my low mood made it sound like my fault. But if I take a responsible attitude towards my depression, then I look at how I can best respond to it. I had become stuck in a recurring pattern of low mood states and I wanted to find out how I could shift this. To do that, I needed to recognize what part I played in the loop.

Understanding loops

With any stuck pattern, there is a loop in time that keeps returning to the same point again and again. This is the 'here I am again' point. Some loops involve a behaviour we keep doing, like smoking, overeating or sabotaging success in an area we have mixed feelings about. Other loops constantly take us back to a situation we've come to know well, like a depressed mood state, familiar argument or recurring drama at work. What behavioural and situational loops have in common is that they keep bringing us back to a place we've been to before. It is the déjà vu feeling of familiarity that defines the loop (see Figure 7.2).

How come
I'm back
here again?

Figure 7.2 Stuck patterns involve repeating loops

We tend to think about behaviours and situations in different ways: behaviours happen *from* people, while situations happen *to* people. If we're stuck in a behavioural loop, we might ask: 'Why do I keep doing this?' For situational loops, the question tends to be: 'Why does this keep happening to me?' The usual assumption is that we cause our own behaviour, but for situations beyond our control we don't have a causal role. This makes us blameworthy for our behaviours but a victim or innocent bystander of situations.

Pattern thinking takes a different approach, assuming that both situations and behaviours have many causes. Personal power opens up when we recognize our role in these. The model of the 3Ps can help us do this.

The 3Ps behind the pattern

Every pattern has three groups of causes. These are the 3Ps of *predisposing, precipitating* and *perpetuating* causes. They act together, like the squares in Figure 7.3, to create the pattern.

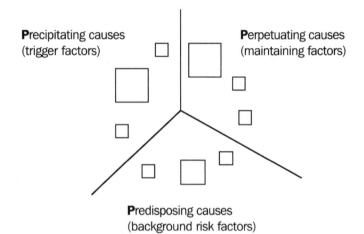

Precipitating causes
(trigger factors)

Perpetuating causes
(maintaining factors)

Predisposing causes
(background risk factors)

Figure 7.3 The 3Ps behind the pattern

Predisposing causes

If a pattern is a scene that keeps repeating, then what sets the scene? What in the background makes it more likely to occur? I think of predisposing causes as the ground from which the pattern emerges. This background includes personal history, cultural context, family upbringing, genetic influences, recent events, diet and many other factors. Some of these are things you can change, others you can't.

Recognizing the role of background can help you become more understanding, and therefore forgiving, of yourself if aspects of your life have turned out differently from how you'd like them to be. It isn't your fault if your genes, early experience or cultural context have installed in you tendencies to react in particular ways. The patterns we get stuck in are often ones we've grown up with and are linked to responses deeply ingrained within us. In spite of our best intentions, we may find ourselves slipping back into an old habit of thought or behaviour again and again. But this is just the starting point. It is possible to turn things around.

We may not choose the cards life deals us, but we can make choices about how we respond. This is finding response-ability.

When giving up my job didn't cure my depression, I went through a painful period of soul searching. I reached the point where I was so fed up with feeling low that I made a decision: if there was to be a way out of this, then I was going to find it. I began to search for insights and strategies that would help me climb out of depression into greater levels of happiness. Just making that decision changed something. A feature had been added to my background that increased my chances of recovery: I was committed to the journey of getting well.

When I started researching depression, I was struck by how common it was. According to a recent editorial in the *British Journal of Psychiatry*,[1] nearly half the population of the western world may suffer an episode at some point in their lives. Over the last 50 years there has been a dramatic rise in the level of depression found in rich industrialized countries, with some studies showing increases as much as tenfold.[2] When a condition is this common, it isn't just a personal problem, it is also a cultural one. There is a shift in thinking when we start recognizing something as a shared issue rather than merely an individual one. Here's an example of what a difference this can make.

Doctors are a group with high rates of depression and are, on average, more likely to commit suicide than their patients.[3] Yet within medical culture there is often a pride that makes it difficult to admit you are finding it difficult to cope. If everyone puts on a brave face, each person gets the impression that everyone else is doing fine. As a result, someone who is struggling is more likely to experience the sense of failure and isolation that feeds depression. In my training and consultancy work with healthcare teams, one of my main roles is to carry out cultural interventions. I explore with teams how they can move from a culture where problems are hidden and people feel alone to one where issues are in the open and they can be dealt with. There is often tremendous relief when we do this.

Culture exists on a personal as well as a collective level, as each of us has our own set of customs and ways of doing things. Some of these we've consciously chosen, others we've picked up from the larger context around us. A stuck pattern is more difficult to change if your personal culture supports the old way of doing things. For example, giving up smoking is harder if you socialize in smoky environments.

Focusing on background factors helps you identify practical steps that support the change you want to make. Each step by itself may not be enough to cure you of the old pattern, but when you add them together, they act as a whole in a way that can shift the balance. The goal here is to create a context that makes success in changing a stuck pattern more likely.

When I made up my mind to move away from depression, I decided to change my personal culture so that it became one that supported increased levels of happiness and emotional health. I started to exercise more, drink less, meditate, manage my stress better, pay attention to diet and give more time to things I enjoyed. I learnt to challenge the types of thinking that made depression more likely, like excessively comparing myself with other people or discounting the value of small steps. I also decided to work fewer hours, have less money and instead develop sources of non-material wealth like clearer purpose, improved relationships and a feeling of connection with life.

These changes didn't all happen at once. But what had changed was my clarity about my values. I knew I didn't want to get stuck in depression again. I began my emotional migration to healthier realms. I'm still taking these steps – the journey never ends – but it is now over 16 years since I was last clinically depressed.

Precipitating causes

Jim told me about a recent argument with his partner. 'She made me so angry,' he said. What he's doing here is identifying his partner as the cause of his anger. She was late, that disturbed his plans and he got furious. But was she really the cause?

If we look at the background, there is much here that helps explain Jim's anger. His father had a similar pattern, so family upbringing and genetics might both play roles. He was also annoyed because his partner was often late and they'd only spoken about it last week. While he was waiting, Jim started to think that she was doing it on purpose just to wind him up. As he hadn't eaten all day, his blood sugar was low and this made him more prone to react angrily. These are some of the *predisposing* causes that set the scene. His partner being late was the trigger factor that tipped him over the edge. That was the *precipitating* cause.

When two things closely follow each other in time, it is easy to think of the first as the cause. But as this example illustrates, trigger factors are only part of the story. The value of focusing on the background is that it gives Jim places he can act to shift his stuck pattern of rage. While he can't change his genetics or upbringing, he could have breakfast; regular healthy meals have a mood-stabilizing effect. He could also notice the thoughts that lead him into angry land and learn to challenge these. The meaning he was giving to lateness was only one of many possible explanations he could have chosen. By addressing background causes, Jim puts himself in a stronger position to deal with triggers without blowing up. However, we can't put everything down to background. Precipitating factors still remain as important causes that need to be addressed. Here's how this can be done.

Jim started to keep a mood diary where he recorded significant events and his reactions to them. While this only took him a few minutes each evening, it subtly changed the way he approached situations. He started to become much more interested in his emotional responses. Like a wildlife enthusiast on the trail of a fascinating creature, Jim began tracking his anger. When did it show itself? What warning signs were there that it was going to appear? And what situations were most likely to draw it out? By becoming a studious observer of himself, Jim found that he was relating *to* his anger rather than *from* it. And with the increased awareness that this brought, he was able to identify the trigger factors that most commonly provoked rageful responses. These were his high-risk situations.

Whenever you get stuck in a particular behaviour, it is worth asking what function this might be attempting to serve. Patterns develop out of learned responses, and the ones that get most strongly established are those that initially seem to work well. Jim's temper had developed as an expression of protest when things were feeling out of control. There were times when this response had stopped unacceptable things happening, like when he'd been bullied at school. But because this had become a deeply ingrained habitual response, it tended to happen by itself rather than through choice, being triggered by the experience of losing control.

To change habitual behaviours, first identify any needs they might be attempting to meet, and then find alternative ways of meeting the need. Each time you feel your pattern triggered, ask yourself: 'What do I really need right now?' If you have a range of ways of meeting your needs, you are less likely to fall back into your old pattern.

Jim needed to find other responses to the feeling of being out of control. He learned to reassure himself that even if things went differently to how he'd planned, he'd be able to cope. Most of the time this worked well. By both tackling the background factors and developing new ways of dealing with the triggers to his loss of temper, he made real progress in changing his pattern.

However, there may be times when in spite of learning new responses you still find yourself falling back into old habits. This is where the next group of causes needs to be tackled: the perpetuating factors.

Perpetuating causes

We usually think of causes as happening *before* the situation or behaviour. If *A* causes *B*, then *A* needs to happen before *B*. What's unusual about perpetuating causes is that they happen *afterwards*.

If someone responds to depression by drinking heavily, they may become more depressed because of the chemical effect of alcohol on the brain. Where the consequence of something is also a cause of it, a loop is created. In this case, it becomes a vicious cycle (see Figure 7.4), where the more they're depressed, the more they drink, the more they drink, the more depressed they become. Drinking and depression become perpetuating causes for each other. In my addictions work I see this happening a lot.

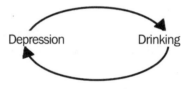

Figure 7.4 A loop where the consequence is also a cause

People often ask: 'Which came first?' Behind this question usually lies an assumption that causes are more important if they come earlier. In practical terms though, the most important causes are the ones we can influence. If there's a loop going on, acting anywhere in it can make a difference. So the focus becomes identifying *choice points*: the points at which our choices influence the way things go. The trouble is, sometimes it seems too easy to make the wrong choice.

Paul went to a party. He'd had a busy few weeks and felt like letting his hair down. He was a bit tense when he got there and had a few drinks to get in a party mood. Someone offered him a cigarette. He didn't smoke; he'd given up two years ago. But then again he was having a night out. He wanted to unwind. So he said 'thank you' and lit up.

That night Paul had a great evening. He also had five cigarettes. And the next day he paid the price: he woke up with nicotine hunger and spent the whole morning wondering whether to buy some tobacco.

A sticky pattern is one that's difficult to shake off, and even when you do you can easily get stuck to it again. Smoking is a good example. What makes it so sticky? Paul's relapse had plenty of predisposing causes. He felt tense and was looking for release; he was at a party and wanted to fit in. In our cultural background, huge amounts of money are spent on advertising images that associate smoking with tension relief and social success. The trigger was being offered a cigarette. That tipped him over the edge. But once he'd started, a whole set of perpetuating causes came into play. He had the thought: 'I've blown it now, I might as well continue.' He fell back into his old identity of thinking of himself as a smoker. And then the next morning he experienced a reawakening of withdrawal symptoms. He had come to a choice point familiar to anyone struggling with addictive behaviour.

Paul's dilemma brings up issues relevant to changing many stuck patterns. On the one hand, he could go down that familiar old route of giving in to temptation. He doesn't like the way he's feeling and smoking offers a quick fix that will relieve his discomfort. But on the other hand, he knows that if he does smoke, the apparent benefit will be short-lived: it won't be long before withdrawal symptoms return and he's back at the same point again. In addition, each cigarette deepens his dependence on nicotine, making future withdrawal symptoms more likely.

There are two different types of loop occurring here. The first is a short-term balancing loop, the second a longer-term amplifying loop. In the balancing type, each journey round the loop reduces tension, bringing Paul back to a state where he feels more in balance. Before the first cigarette at the party, he felt on edge. When he lit up, he felt as if he was joining in more and his social anxiety fell away. This happened at several points in the evening. The next morning, smoking also appeared to offer Paul a form of tension relief, so the shape of the loop is similar (see Figure 7.5). Tension increases the temptation to smoke, and smoking temporarily reduces the tension.

Figure 7.5 Short term – a balancing loop reducing tension

In the longer term, however, each journey round the loop makes future tension from withdrawal symptoms more likely. This amplifying loop leads to the sort of vicious cycle that keeps someone hooked (see Figure 7.6).

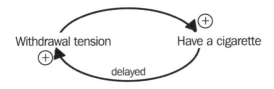

Figure 7.6 Long term – an amplifying loop increasing tension

These two loops explain the paradox that although most smokers believe that smoking helps them relax, people who smoke tend to become more anxious. The tension goes but it comes back with interest. The same thing happens with heavy drinking and depression. In the short term drinking offers relief by blotting out problems, but in the long term it adds to them. As the problems pile up, they become more difficult to face, making further drinking an even more tempting option.

I call this the whirlpool effect (see Figure 7.7). Whatever starts the pattern off, once it gets going it perpetuates itself in a downward spiral that sucks people in.

Figure 7.7 The whirlpool effect

What we're looking at here is how some patterns get stuck because they cause themselves to happen more. Wherever the consequence of something is also a cause of it, an amplifying loop is created that can keep the pattern going. In practical terms, this makes it important to look at what happens after the 'here I am again' moment. The aim is to identify any responses or consequences that make the pattern more likely to keep occurring. Here are some other examples:

◆ *After becoming depressed, Carol doesn't feel like going out. Social isolation and physical inactivity then make her depression worse.*

◆ *Feeling hurt after a row, each partner reacts with hostility to the other. This adds to the hurt they feel, making future rows more likely.*

◆ *An organization has such a poor working atmosphere that staff leave. As turnover is so high, the relationships needed for teamwork don't develop.*

The essence of finding your power is recognizing that whatever the situation you face, you always have choices about how you respond. When your response to a stuck pattern is a decision to change it, a turning point occurs. You start a journey. There are stages to this and tools that help. Using the principles we've looked at so far, here's a simple, practical process for shifting stuck patterns.

Become the change

The first stage of change is simply to become aware of an issue, concern or opportunity you want to give your attention to. A tool that can help this is the review stage of the dream cycle. If there's a stuck pattern you'd like to change, you can begin this process now by bringing it into view.

Review 1: Bring the pattern into view
Complete the following open-ended sentences:

◆ *The pattern I'd like to change is...*
◆ *Attractions of this pattern, or functions it may serve, include...*
◆ *The reasons I want to change this pattern include...*

It is important to acknowledge the attractions the pattern may have. If it serves a function, then part of you may be unwilling to let it go. For example, if smoking, drinking or playing computer games is used as a way of unwinding or rewarding yourself, then stopping these things, or even cutting them down, may be seen as a loss rather than a gain. Once you've identified the purposes your pattern serves, you can develop other ways of meeting those needs.

When habits resist attempts to change them, at some level, whether conscious or unconscious, there's likely to be an ambivalence blocking progress. Facing and working through mixed feelings is therefore an essential part of the change process. Without it, any use of clever techniques is likely to be sabotaged.

The way to deal with ambivalence is to bring it into the open. When fears of change lie under the surface, they can lead to unconscious resistance. By moving them into conscious view, you can assess any threats your anxieties are based on and use problem-solving approaches to deal with these.

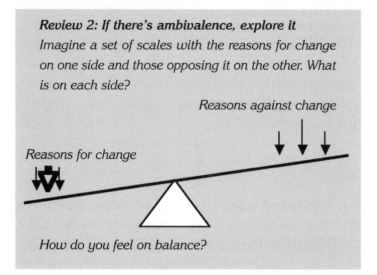

Review 2: If there's ambivalence, explore it
Imagine a set of scales with the reasons for change on one side and those opposing it on the other. What is on each side?

Reasons against change

Reasons for change

How do you feel on balance?

Sticky patterns usually have short-term benefits but long-term costs. Moving out of a stuck state tends to involve effort at first, but for benefits that come later. If you're to motivate yourself through that initial difficult transition period, you need compelling reasons. To break the spell of a stuck state, look at where your pattern is taking you. Is this where you want to go?

It's often dissatisfaction that initially drives habit change, but for letting go to last, the old needs to be replaced with something new. Otherwise a vacuum is left that can easily be filled with a return to the old loop. What would be so good that it would be worth giving up the old pattern for? The dream stage can help here.

Dream: Identify a positive vision to head for
Imagine that you have succeeded in moving on from your old pattern. What are the best things about this? Thinking about the benefits of change gives you a positive vision to head for.

If you know what you've had enough of but you're not sure what to replace it with, don't let that stop you changing. If you've a concern that's motivating you, act on it. One of the most important acts in any journey of change is making a decision. What are you going to do with your pattern? What is your intention?

Plan 1: Make your decision
◆ *My decision is that I will...*
◆ *The reasons I'm determined about this include...*

Intention is what follows decision. It is where you are so committed to a course of action that you're able to say 'I will...' and mean it. Intentions and decisions can be deepened. You can feed them. Here's how you can do this.

Plan 2: Deepen determination
◆ *First of all, rate your current level of determination on a 1–10 scale.*

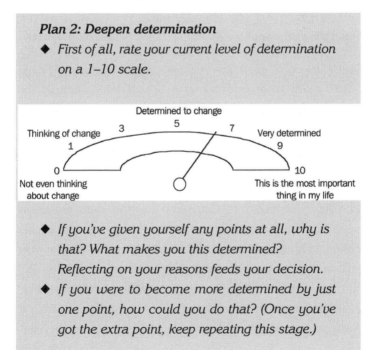

◆ *If you've given yourself any points at all, why is that? What makes you this determined?*
  Reflecting on your reasons feeds your decision.
◆ *If you were to become more determined by just one point, how could you do that? (Once you've got the extra point, keep repeating this stage.)*

Your decision, intention and level of determination are parts of the background that influence the likelihood of change. You could argue that they are the most important parts. For each of them your choices make a difference, and without them the pattern is likely to remain stuck. There is something else in the background that is important too – your level of confidence that you can succeed in shifting this pattern.

Plan 3: Deepen confidence

◆ *First of all, rate your current level of confidence on a 1–10 scale.*

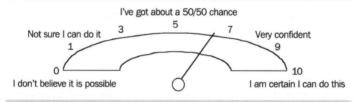

◆ *If you've given yourself any points at all, why is that? What makes you this confident? Naming your strengths is a way of reinforcing them.*

◆ *If you were to become more confident by just one point, how could you do that? (Once you've got the extra point, keep repeating this stage.)*

If you've scored less than five on the determination scale, it could be that you're not ready to make this change yet. It might be the wrong time or maybe you still have doubts. You can increase determination by finding, or creating, more compelling reasons. For example, making a commitment to someone who'll notice if you don't stick to a change is a way of increasing its importance. It also brings in a supporting relationship in a way that can help confidence.

You'll notice that a lot of attention is being given to preparation. If you focus on changes you're convinced you want to make, you can save yourself from the repeated failures that tend to happen when you haven't got your heart in something. Although most people make New Year's resolutions, around 50 per cent of these are abandoned by the end of January.[4] The time given to getting clear about what you want helps set you up for more likely success.

If you're determined to make a change and your confidence is strong, then go ahead and make it. But if you don't rate your chances too highly, then you need the next stage of planning: the research phase. Many things seem impossible before you learn how to do them, so don't be surprised if your confidence is low when you take on a challenge that stretches you. The first stage in finding a way is wanting to. If you have some determination behind you, then you're already part way there. The research phase involves seeking out the skills, insights and resources needed to succeed.

The simplest form of research is just noticing what happens. If you're concerned about a pattern of overeating, pay special attention to the times when this occurs. What's the background to these events? Are there triggers that set it off? And how do you respond once it has happened?

Plan 4: The research phase
◆ *What do you need to learn or develop in order to shift this pattern?*

> ◆ *When it happens, what are the*
>   *– background factors?*
>   *– trigger factors?*
>   *– perpetuating factors?*
> ◆ *Who do you know who's successfully shifted a pattern like this? How did they do it?*

When people try to stop themselves doing something, they often feel guilty when they fail. Yet feeling bad about yourself may be a trigger that provokes further episodes of the same pattern. What's great about the research phase is that it turns occasions of relapse into opportunities for learning. Rather than thinking 'I'm such an idiot, why am I doing this again?' move out of self-condemnation and into curiosity. What set it off this time? And more importantly, how are you going to respond?

Each time you fall into the old pattern, you're given the chance to practise different ways of getting out of it again. Here's a method you can use for this. It's an example of a *pattern interrupt* strategy. When you're using techniques like this, you've moved out of planning and into the *do* stage of the dream cycle.

> **Do 1: The inner traffic light technique**
> ◆ *As soon as you notice yourself slipping into an old pattern again, imagine yourself looking at a red traffic light and say the word 'STOP'.*
> ◆ *Ask yourself: 'Is this what I really want to be doing?' If it isn't, picture the light turning to amber as you think of a simple, positive, achievable goal to head for (it doesn't matter what it is, as your intention is just to shift track).*

> ◆ *Once you've identified a target to head for, picture the traffic light turning green and say the word 'GO'. Head for your new goal.*
> ◆ *Each time you succeed in shifting track, celebrate your mini-victory.*

As you gain more confidence in your ability to shift track, you can get to do this at earlier stages. Eventually you can learn to pick up warning signs when you're heading off course, acting in advance to prevent the old pattern returning.

Finding ways of staying on the case is an essential element in maintaining any change. It is here that much can be learnt from the sticky patterns themselves. The patterns that are most difficult to give up are those that are self-reinforcing. They make themselves happen more. The same principles can be applied to the change you want to make. For it to last, it needs to reinforce itself.

One way of doing this is to make sure that you notice and appreciate the steps you take that you feel good about. This takes us back to the review stage.

> ### Review: What do I feel good about?
> *Each time you take a step that supports the change you want to make, find a way of acknowledging that. Congratulate yourself. When you feel good about what you've done, you're more likely to continue to do it.*

Many people fail in their attempts to shift stuck patterns because they don't have the tools. The good news is that even the most sticky behaviours and situations can change. The tools introduced so far go a long way to equipping you with what you need to be successful. But there is still a vital ingredient missing, which you'll need when taking on the most difficult challenges. The next chapter introduces what this is.

Power points

1 If an unwelcome habit or situation keeps recurring in your life, then you have a stuck pattern you might want to change. You can use the dream cycle to help you do this.

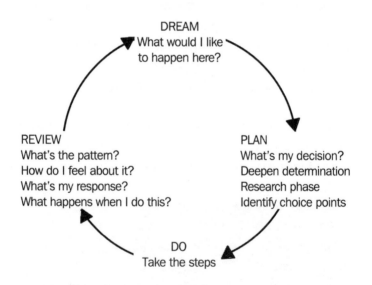

DREAM
What would I like
to happen here?

PLAN
What's my decision?
Deepen determination
Research phase
Identify choice points

DO
Take the steps

REVIEW
What's the pattern?
How do I feel about it?
What's my response?
What happens when I do this?

2 Many patterns get stuck because they have short-term benefits but long-term costs. This can lead to part of you wanting change and part of you resisting it. Working through mixed feelings is therefore an essential part of the change process. Look at both sides of the argument and then decide which way you want to go.

3 It is easy to blame yourself or others if you attempt to change but fail. Rather than looking back in time for someone to point a finger at, look forward and ask yourself: 'Which way do I want to go and how can I take steps in that direction?' This helps you move from blame to response-ability.

4 You find your power to shift stuck patterns by recognizing choice points. These are the places where your choices and actions can help steer you out of the old loop. Knowing about the 3Ps helps you find these.

◆ **Predisposing causes**: what in the background makes the pattern more likely? Which of these factors can you change?

◆ **Precipitating causes**: what trigger factors can you identify? How can you deal with these?

◆ **Perpetuating causes**: what keeps the pattern going once it has started? What can you do to change this?

5 Celebrate every mini-victory along the path. If you feel good about the steps you're taking, you'll be more likely to keep taking them.

8

Bouncing Back from Failure and Crisis

*I*n the spring of 1989, while on holiday in Scotland, I momentarily fell asleep while driving. When I opened my eyes I found myself on the wrong side of the road with a car speeding towards me. Swerving to miss it, I went off the road. My car span out of control and I crashed into a rock face. My vehicle was a complete write-off, but miraculously I escaped unharmed. Although I could easily have been killed, I look back on that event as one of the most important in my life. In many ways, I even feel grateful that it happened.

At the time I had been working as a junior doctor for several years. Just seven days previously I'd finished a working week of 112 hours. The crash served as a wake-up call because it mirrored what was happening in my life. When you drive yourself on and on without adequate rest, you're likely to crash. I knew that, unless I changed, I was heading for another disaster.

I got the message. The first thing I did when I returned from my holiday was hand in my resignation. With the depression I felt back then, my life had gone sour. Getting out of that job was the starting point of my recovery.

My car crash is an example of how something that seems awful at the time may later become valued as a turning point. I see this in my addictions work too, where recovery often begins with the crisis of hitting bottom. But such awfulness doesn't always lead to improvement. Why do some disasters strengthen us while others feed a downward spiral?

I've been studying this question for over a decade and have identified 10 bounce-back principles that can make a difference. This chapter introduces these, showing how they can help you get up after the falls and face failure or crisis in ways that leave you strengthened.

The 10 bounce-back principles are:

- *See failure as an inevitable part of life.*
- *The way to succeed is to double your failure rate.*
- *Turn a minus into a plus.*
- *PO: a tool for creative thinking.*
- *When it hurts say 'ouch'.*
- *Forgiveness.*
- *Use the dream cycle.*
- *Learn to change your state.*
- *I can't, we can.*
- *Trust in something larger than yourself.*

See failure as an inevitable part of life

Although it may sound like negative thinking, this insight forms a central part of the bounce-back approach. Some positive thinkers say 'Don't even think about failure'; I find it more useful to look at *how* you think about failure, as it is this that makes such a difference to your ability to get up after a fall.

When failing is viewed as a bad thing that must be avoided, two common response patterns occur. The first is *challenge avoidance*, where someone avoids taking risks. In the short term this protects them from failure, as they shy away from doing things that might go wrong. In the long term, however, it stunts the development of real confidence, as there is no opportunity for meaningful success or the learning that comes when things go wrong.

The second response is *challenge attack*, where the idea of failing is so unacceptable that someone works furiously hard to ensure that it never happens. People with this approach often seem successful, but tend to pay a price for this. Because they don't have the option of admitting defeat, they are more likely to struggle on when facing situations that seem impossible. Being squeezed between a *must* and a *can't* (Figure 8.1) creates enormous psychological pressure, bringing an increased risk of stress-related illness.

Figure 8.1 Squeezed between a must and a can't

Challenge avoidance and challenge attack are both expressions of the fight or flight response. Fleeing from any possibility of failure leads to avoidance. Declaring war on failure makes life a battleground so driven by the anxiety of things going wrong that it's hard to enjoy what you're doing. And when things do fall apart, if someone finds failing hard to accept, the real danger is that they try to cover it up, denying that there's any problem. Cover-ups might work as a short-term fix for embarrassment, but over time they make problems worse, as future decisions become based on false information rather than reality.

If failure is regarded as an inevitable feature of life, it can be accepted without shame. When it happens, you don't need to deny it or feel you are a bad person because of it. Notice this isn't about becoming blasé. Personal power involves being clear about what you'd like to happen. But when things work out differently, you need a way of looking that enhances your capacity to respond rather than blocks it.

So the first bounce-back principle is simply to accept that failure is part of the landscape of life. You take steps to prevent it, but when it happens it doesn't destroy you. You can then develop a response that helps you get back on course. The key point here is this: it's not whether you fail but how you respond when you do fail that makes the biggest difference to longer-term success.

The way to succeed is to double your failure rate

Each time you fail at something, there are reasons for it. If you were fully aware of these beforehand, you probably would have done better. It is through failing that you come to know more about the challenges you're facing.

Each failure can teach you something new. This is such an important approach to learning that Japanese industry has coined a word for it – *kaizen*, which means continuous improvement. The motto of kaizen is: 'Every defect is a jewel because it points the way towards continuous improvement.' Each failure or setback alerts you to areas where adjustments are needed. This approach has been credited with being a major factor in helping Japanese industry develop its reputation for reliability.

The key insight here is that when you see failure not as a bad thing associated with shame but as a learning opportunity, then it can become part of your training for later success (see Figure 8.2). Thomas Watson, the founder of IBM, recognized this when he said: 'The way to succeed is to double your failure rate.'

Figure 8.2 Mistakes can help you make good decisions

Thomas Edison failed thousands of times in his attempts to get the electric light bulb to work. Someone asked him how he could keep going when his idea was so obviously failing. He replied: 'I am not discouraged, because every wrong attempt discarded is another step forward.' You won't know that something isn't going to work unless you try it. The term for this is negative research. Each blind alley explored, each option investigated, adds to the experience that prepares you to succeed.

You can look at failure in various ways and give different meanings to it. If you see each slip-up as evidence that you are hopeless, then you are giving failure a meaning that blocks your personal power. This is static thinking (see Figure 8.3).

I am a failure. This is the way I am. I'm just one of those people who always messes up. It will always be like this. That last disaster just proves it.

Figure 8.3 A static thinking approach to failure

If you view your mess-ups as evidence that you are courageous enough to try something new or difficult, then you give failure a very different meaning. How do you see failure? Does the meaning you give to it block you or encourage you?

Try this: Exploring what failure means to you
What naturally follows these open-ended sentences for you?
◆ *If I fail, it means...*
◆ *What I don't like about failing is...*
◆ *What I like about failing is...*

Turn a minus into a plus

It may seem strange to be looking at what you like about failing. I encourage you to do this because bouncing back is easier if you can see the positive side of your defeat. When you look for the value in what has happened and can see some advantages, it takes the sting out of failing.

When you find yourself in a really awful situation, it may not be you who has failed. Rather, it can feel like life has failed you. Yet even in the most ghastly of scenarios, it may be possible to find some value. This can be a survival strategy that stops you feeling completely ground down by adversity. It is a way of retaining an inner strength.

When the Austrian psychiatrist Viktor Frankl was interned in Auschwitz, he held in his mind a positive vision of how he could use this experience. He imagined himself giving lectures on the psychology of concentration camps. By doing this, he changed the meaning he attached to what he went through. It gave him a purpose to live for. Even though he lost his wife, parents and brother in the camps, he was determined to draw out lessons we could all benefit from. After the war, he did go on to lecture around the world. His books have been hugely influential, one of them selling over two million copies.[1]

> **Try this: Finding value**
> ◆ *What do you find most difficult in your life?*
> ◆ *Are there ways in which dealing with this has strengthened you? Perhaps lessons you've learnt or qualities you've developed?*

If you've had a personal hell, you don't have to be glad that it happened. But one of the ways of creating a turnaround is to use whatever life offers you so that some benefit comes out of it. What happens is what happens. It is in your response that you find your power.

PO: A tool for creative thinking

Humans have been described as creatures of habit, and once we've settled into a particular way of doing things we're unlikely to change unless we've got good reasons to. PO is a word coined by Edward de Bono[2] to describe something that stops you in your tracks in a way that encourages you to consider a wider range of options. The letters PO stand for provocative operation, and PO refers to anything that provokes you to think more laterally. Crisis, failure and disappointments serve as very effective POs, as it is the bumps in life that most often jolt us into rethinking things. When the rethink leads to a better way of doing things, then the crisis gets remembered as a turning point.

My car crash is a good example of this. It jolted me into awareness, leading to a change of course in my life direction. But we don't have to wait till we bump into something before re-evaluating. All you need do is ask yourself: 'Why am I doing what I'm doing?' Is it out of habit, because everyone else does, or because you've got good reasons?

When it hurts, say 'ouch'

Disappointments and setbacks occur when reality works out differently from how you'd like it to. When this happens, it often hurts. That pain tells you that what you were hoping for was important to you. It also alerts you to the fact that your expectations were inaccurate.

Just as you might come out in a physical bruise when you have a bad knock, when it hurts after a big disappointment it is useful to think of yourself as having an emotional bruise. You grieve for the loss of how you would like things to have been. This grieving is part of how you adjust to a new reality.

If you were to fall and break your leg, it would hurt a lot. That pain tells you there's an injury that needs your attention. If you didn't feel the pain, you might continue walking on the leg in a way that did further damage or prevented it healing properly. When you have an injury, you need recovery time in order to restore normal function. It is the same with emotional bruising and psychological injuries. When you feel pain, ask yourself: 'What do I need in order to promote recovery?'

What we're looking at here is what will help you get back on your feet again after a fall. If it is painful, you may need some recovery time to recharge before facing the next challenge. But just like a baby learning to walk, don't let the falls put you off.

Forgiveness

In my work in the addictions field, I sometimes come across people who've done such awful things when drinking that they hate themselves. If you've ever done something you see as really bad, valuing your mistakes as learning opportunities may not feel quite enough. How can we move on from the memories that make us squirm inside with shame? Something extra is needed here: forgiveness.

You forgive yourself by consciously choosing to let go of the belief that you are a bad person who deserves to be punished. This may seem a dramatic statement, but the idea that you are a bad person is not always a conscious one. Even if on the surface you quite like yourself, you can have degrees of self-hate and harsh self-judgement lurking deep inside your mind. The tell-tale signs are when you set yourself overly punishing schedules, feel tormented inside or sabotage yourself from getting what you really want because on some level you feel you don't deserve it.

One approach to forgiveness is simply to forget. The problem with this is that it blocks learning from experience. A mistake is more likely to be repeated if you haven't acknowledged and learnt from it. So how else can you forgive yourself?

I find it useful to think of forgiveness as a process that involves a number of stages. The first one is recognizing when you've done something you don't feel good about. It is important to be quite specific here about what it is you've done that you feel was wrong. The second stage is to feel uncomfortable (or guilty) about this. That discomfort provides the inspirational dissatisfaction to motivate the third stage: a clear decision to change. This change involves a conscious turning away from the behaviour you feel bad about. For example, if you'd lost your temper and hit someone you care about, the decision might be to learn about anger management or non-violent approaches to dealing with conflict.

Forgiveness starts as soon as you've made the commitment to change – but it also grows the more you act on that decision. As you build up new memories of actions that are more in line with your values, you feel the guilt disappearing. You don't need to carry it any more, it has served its purpose. Some time later, you might look back on the incident you felt bad about and see it as a turning point, as the start of a new way.

Use the dream cycle

So far we've been looking mostly at ways of picking yourself up after falls and failings. But what about the times when *everything* goes wrong, the times of disaster and crisis?

The dream cycle is a useful tool here because it offers a structure that can be applied to any situation. The short form adapted for emergency use would go like this:

1 *Review – What's going on? How am I doing? What are my concerns?*
2 *Dream – What would I like to happen here?*
3 *Plan – How can I take steps to move that way?*
4 *Do – Take the steps.*
5 *Review – Any changes? Back to the top.*

If you don't currently have a crisis in your life, it is still worth applying the dream cycle, but using it to look at your capacity for responding to crisis.

A basic principle of fire safety is preparation: thinking in advance about how you might respond if a fire were to occur. In the middle of an emergency, it can be difficult suddenly to invent a plan from scratch. But if you've considered issues beforehand and developed a drill that is easy to follow, this can save anguish and lives. Similar principles can be applied to crises in general. It is reasonably likely that at some points in your life you will find yourself in extreme situations that push you beyond your limits. Deaths, accidents, breakdown of relationships and organizations, awful things do happen. How confident do you feel in your ability to deal with times like this?

When someone is injured, those with first aid training are less likely to get in a spin and more likely to be able to rise to the challenge of responding constructively. In a similar way, if you've thought about some of the issues that come up when facing a crisis and have worked out ways to respond to them, you're more likely to be able to rise to the challenge when you need to. So how can you prepare? Let's start by reviewing what it is that makes something a crisis.

The *Concise Oxford Dictionary* gives two definitions of crisis: a time of danger and a turning point. However, the term is more commonly used to refer to any extreme situation that we're having difficulty coping with. It can describe a huge range of circumstances, from feeling alarmed about an approaching deadline all the way through to the threat of war or ecological breakdown. What these situations have in common is that to the person experiencing them, they feel beyond the range of what is normally manageable. They take us over the edge.

Something that might be a crisis for one person may not be for another. If a water pipe burst in my home, I might experience this as a crisis. But if I was a plumber, I'd just get on and fix it. I tend to think 'crisis over' when I've found a way of managing the situation.

What we're looking at here are two different aspects of crisis – the first is the situation itself, in terms of how extreme or dangerous it is, and the second is our ability to respond to it (see Figure 8.4). The importance of recognizing this second aspect is that it is something we can change. Our coping ability varies from day to day, depending on what state we're in.

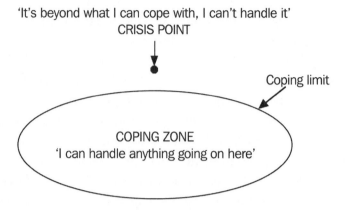

Figure 8.4 Crisis points are outside our coping zone

The dream cycle is a general-purpose tool that can be applied to any type of change. So if you'd like to increase your ability to deal with extreme events, first start at the *review* stage. Take a look at your life and consider what sort of difficult events you might encounter. What is your current level of confidence at being able to deal with these? What strengths do you have that would help you? Then move into *dream* by asking yourself how you'd like to be able to respond. What sort of strengths or skills would you like to develop? *Planning* involves looking at how you can do this, how you can train yourself. After identifying steps you can take, the *do* phase involves doing them. Continue the cycle by *reviewing* progress, both to acknowledge the areas where you feel your confidence growing and to keep track of the gaps you'd like to fill.

By using the dream cycle like this, you strengthen your capacity to deal with challenging events. Thinking of potential difficulties before they happen, you can prepare yourself so that if a crisis occurs, you're better placed to face it and bounce back afterwards. Like an insurance policy you hope you'll never use, when or if disaster strikes you'll be glad you made the effort. What you also do is address any underlying anxieties you have by naming the situations you fear and identifying ways to handle them. As you do this, you may notice your general confidence grow.

With crisis planning, a question that comes up is how you work out which threats are appropriate to prepare for and which ones are far fetched. Anxiety can certainly feed on itself in a way that blows risks out of proportion. But the opposite can also happen, as denial and complacency turn mountains into molehills. What can be said with greater certainty is that crisis occurs. Like failure, it is part of the landscape. So it is worth thinking about how you deal with it. The next principle can help here.

Learn to change your state

If your ability to deal with crisis depends on what state you're in, how do you move out of not-so-capable states into more resourceful ones? This question points to one of the key ways of improving bounce-back ability. And the starting point is to recognize that extreme situations can push people either way. We can fall into shock, panic, defeat or denial. But crisis can also evoke powerfully engaged and creative states, and when this happens we tend to feel strengthened by difficult circumstances as well as more intensely alive during them.

Because shock, panic, defeat and denial are common responses to crisis, I'm going to focus on these first. I'll then look at how you can move out of these into more powerful states.

Shock

When you first hear a piece of disturbing information, it's
a shock to your system. I think of cartoon characters who've
just been whacked on the head with a hammer: their head
vibrates and they feel dazed. They may not know what's hit
them, but they know that something has. This is how shock
can feel. You may experience a sudden loss of energy, the
world appearing somehow distant and unreal.

In the first stage of shock, the main feeling is usually
emptiness or numbness. The information hasn't fully
sunk in. As it does, you may move into the second stage of
shock, recoil. This is like an emotional bruise that comes
out a while after the main impact. It can hurt. You may
even feel sick or tearful.

Think of shock as an adjustment time. You may need
to step back and come to terms with a new situation
before marshalling your energies to face challenge again.

Panic

Panic involves an activation of the body's emergency
'fight and flight' response. What's useful about this is that
if there is a threat, it has been acknowledged in a way that
mobilizes you to respond. A person in panic is unlikely to
complacently leaf through old papers deciding which to
save if their house is on fire – they get out quick.

The downside of the panic response is that it can get
out of control, leading to such a high state of arousal and
alarm that this interferes with effective functioning.
Thoughts race round in circles and anxieties become
blown out of proportion. In severe panic states, abnor-
mally fast breathing (hyperventilation) can lead to a
chemical imbalance in the blood that affects the nervous
system and brain. This causes pins and needles in the fin-

gers as well as a light-headedness that can make it difficult to think clearly. These changes tend to make panic worse, creating a self-amplifying loop (see Figure 8.5). What starts as a minor worry can escalate into a full-blown panic attack.

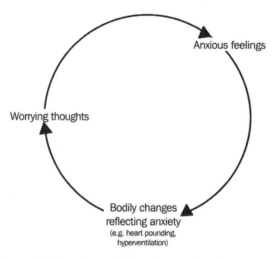

Figure 8.5 A self-amplifying loop of panic

The good news is that once you realize what's going on, you can develop strategies for interrupting the loop and returning to a more balanced state. Here are three strategies you can use.

> **Try this: Strategies for stepping out of panic**
>
> *1 THE THERAPEUTIC PAUSE BUTTON*
>
> *When things are whizzing round too quickly in your mind and you find yourself in a spin, press the pause button. You can do this by simply shifting your attention away from the source of the panic towards something less disturbing.*

Ground yourself in the present moment by asking yourself:

◆ *What am I seeing? (Look around you.)*
◆ *What am I hearing? (How many sounds can you hear?)*
◆ *What can I smell? (Take a big sniff.)*
◆ *What can I taste? (Allow your tongue to wander round your mouth.)*
◆ *What can I feel in my body? (What sensations can you feel?)*

Once you are more settled, you can review the situation in front of you.

2 DIAPHRAGMATIC BREATHING

In panic, breathing occurs more from the shoulders than the belly. You can restore a more relaxed pattern of breathing by:

◆ *Putting one hand on your upper chest and the other over your belly button. See which is moving most. Anxious breathing tends to be more from the top.*

You shift the balance by:

◆ *Breathing in by pushing the lower hand out with your belly (this sucks air into the lungs). Breathe out. Keep repeating this so that you breathe more from the belly than the upper chest.*

3 DO A PERSPECTIVE CHECK ON THINKING

In panic, small problems can get blown out of proportion. Write down the thoughts you have when you're worried. Now ask yourself:

◆ *Am I being overly pessimistic?*
◆ *Are there other ways of looking at this?*

The aim of these panic-interruption strategies is to bring yourself back into a clearer-headed space. Then you can look at ways of responding to the source of your concerns. However, if the problem is too big or you don't have effective problem-solving strategies, the danger is that you can slip into the next state.

Defeat

When I'm counselling people, I pay attention to their posture and the look in their eyes. When someone is in touch with enthusiasm, they sit up, there's glee in their face and a shine in their eyes. In defeat, the opposite occurs. Their body slumps, they don't move much and their eyes are downcast. In this state, life feels like a deep pit and it may seem that nothing you can do will make any difference. This is the inner power cut where the lights of inspiration and possibility have gone out. It's a horrible place to be, and it's a common response to feeling overwhelmed by crisis.

When you're in this state, there are three things to remember. First, when you're in it everything looks bleak (see Figure 8.6). Like viewing the world through dark glasses, all the colour seems to have been taken out. It's therefore not the best place from which to face a crisis.

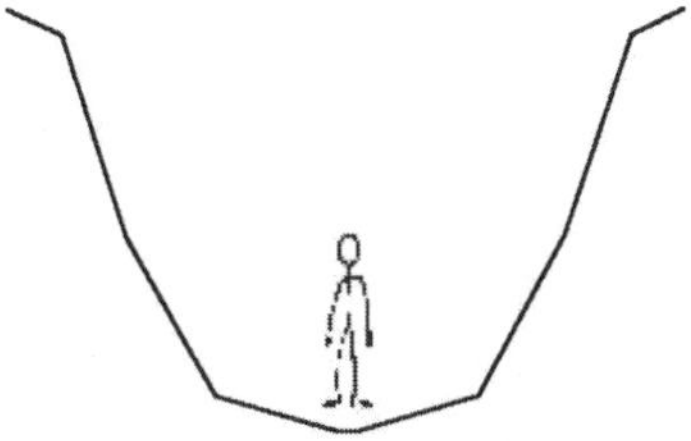

I just can't see a way out of
here. There's no point in
even trying.

Figure 8.6 A state of defeat

It is, however, a good time to remember the second thing, which is the bounce-back principle of turn a minus into a plus. If you look for the value in something, you're more likely to find it. This is even true of the pits of defeat. What's going on in these dark holes is mourning and grief, as there's something that's not working out the way you want it to. When you give expression to your loss, it can help you move on from it. Pits are great places for shedding and letting go, particularly of unrealistic expectations and ways of doing things that weren't working. Allowing aspects of your old reality to die makes room for the birth of something new. The pit is the place to bury what's dead – only don't get stuck there.

That's why you need to remember the third thing: defeat is not a permanent state (although with static thinking it will feel that way). You can move in and out of it.

There are a number of paths out of defeat and I'd like to look at two of these. The first one seems like an easy way out, though really it is just a corridor leading back into the pit and so keeps you trapped. This is the state of denial. The second, which I shall describe afterwards, is engagement. That is the path of personal power.

Denial

A piece of advice sometimes given to people when they are in defeat is: 'Don't worry about things you can't do anything about. Just don't think about them, pretend they're not there.' Compared with the discomfort of defeat, a state of denial can seem very attractive. I'm sure we all need to step back from the difficulty of challenge from time to time. But there is a big difference between temporarily pressing the therapeutic pause button while you recharge, and putting a long-term hold on viewing the bits of reality you don't like.

On the surface, someone in a state of denial may appear to be fine. They sound quite happy with their lives and the state of the world. The difficulty they will eventually face is that problems that are denied don't get dealt with, they accumulate. Crisis remains unaddressed and it grows.

I recently ran a group session exploring ways of dealing with crisis at the addictions treatment unit where I work. One man there said that he didn't have any crisis in his life, implying that the session wasn't relevant for him. Looking at him, I could see that he was deeply jaundiced. He had severe alcoholic liver disease and had recently been told that if he carried on drinking, he might only have a few months left to live. He was clearly in a state of denial.

If someone has never had any training or preparation for dealing with crisis, they may feel overwhelmed when they first confront it. Blotting out problems can seem attractive because it offers instant relief from the emotional upheaval brought on by disturbing realities. If this quick fix appears to work well, the risk is that it becomes a habitual response. Retreating into denial creates a comfort trap, where the more the person avoids reality, the more difficult it becomes to face (see Figure 8.7).

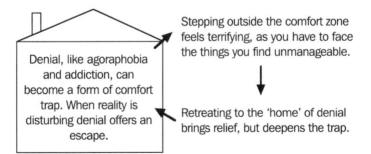

Stepping outside the comfort zone feels terrifying, as you have to face the things you find unmanageable.

Denial, like agoraphobia and addiction, can become a form of comfort trap. When reality is disturbing denial offers an escape.

Retreating to the 'home' of denial brings relief, but deepens the trap.

Figure 8.7 A vicious cycle of denial

The cycle of denial isn't only found in people with drink and drug problems. It can be seen in responses to crisis at a wide range of levels. For example, during the BSE crisis in Britain, the UK government deliberately withheld information from the public because it didn't want people to panic. Ministers publicly ate hamburgers in attempts to reassure everyone, but the government's own inquiry later admitted: 'Ministers followed an approach whose object was sedation.'[3] Something similar happened in the United States recently, when a senior White House official was found to have altered government scientific reports on climate change.[4] Sections were deleted and wording changed, so that the seriousness of the problem was downplayed.

Any training preparing people to deal with crisis needs to warn them about both the temptations and the dangers of denial. Once you recognize the trap you can take steps to get out of it. Doing so may feel uncomfortable at first, in the same way that giving up smoking is. You have to face disturbance in the short term in order to prevent it getting worse in the long term. The alternative is to carry on the downward spiral.

If things do continue to get worse, there is another way out of the denial trap. In addictions recovery this is described as hitting bottom.

> Pete, an alcoholic man in his 30s, recently got badly beaten up. He was taken to hospital and admitted to intensive care. He thought he was going to die. Yet telling me about this some weeks later, he said: 'I'm grateful to the guy who did it, I could shake him by the hand.'

> *What he'd experienced in hospital was a deep-level shift. He'd been so shocked by his close encounter with death that he'd taken a hard look at his life, and seen the direction he was going in. He saw that his drinking was leading him into increasingly dangerous situations and he didn't want to die. He said: 'Lying in intensive care on the edge of death was wake-up call massive.' He made a decision. He wanted to change.*

With hitting bottom, it is not just that something awful happens. It is the way you respond to the awfulness that creates the turning point. Rather than shutting out feelings of alarm, you experience them in a way that leads you to question your old approach. Sadly, that didn't happen with the jaundiced man in my group. It was his lack of alarm, as much as anything else, that led to his continued drinking and eventual death some months later.

Allowing yourself to be disturbed is an essential part of the bounce-back response to crisis. When you feel the horror, this becomes the 'wake-up call massive' that inspires you to rise and face the challenge. This leads to the next state.

Engagement

Engagement begins the moment you make a decision to face and tackle the crisis in front of you. You may not know exactly what you're going to do, but you do have a clear and committed intention to do something. This is hearing your call to adventure and choosing to answer it.

Once you start out on this journey of an active response, you will probably notice a change within you. There may be a renewed sense of purpose, an experience of energy.

You are likely to feel more awake and alive. People in this state tend to feel less fear even though they have accepted the reality of danger. As psychologist and author Dr Susan Jeffers[5] writes in her book *Feel the Fear and Do It Anyway*: 'To become involved is to reduce your fear.'

If you're committed to making the best response you can to a crisis, then it starts to become important to you what state you're in. And in order to get to where you want to go, you need to start from where you are. So the next stage in changing your state is simply to notice what your starting point is. When you have that 'hit on the head with a hammer' feeling, you can gently say to yourself: 'OK, I seem to be in shock.' You can't bounce back from a crisis unless you've noticed it. And noticing your reactions is part of this.

By reviewing how you are and then asking yourself how you'd like to be, you apply the dream cycle to yourself. What you're doing here is recognizing that an essential part of responding to any crisis is getting yourself in a good position to do this. And the way in to a more engaged state is to give yourself a purpose that you believe is achievable. Focusing on changing your state gives you such a purpose.

So how would you like to be able to respond? Picture yourself doing that. Anthony Robbins,[6] who has written extensively about changing states, suggests:

> *Whatever your goal may be, if you create in your mind a clear image of the result you want and represent it to yourself as if you've already achieved it then you will go into the kind of states that will support you in creating the results you desire.*

He also suggests two central mechanisms for changing your state: first to focus on what's happening in your body, and second to act at the level of your communications with yourself. Let's look at these.

Can you remember a time when, facing a challenge, you felt fully engaged and in touch with your personal power? Imagine yourself back there. Re-experience the event as if it were happening right now. Your body will have memories of this moment. Tap into those stored remembrances and recall what it feels like to be with your power. How do you breath? How do you walk? What is your posture? When you're fully engaged, your body is configured differently to how it is when you're slumped in defeat. By reinhabiting the physical expression of engagement, you bring yourself more into this state.

> **Try this: Embodying personal power**
> To use this approach, ask yourself two questions:
> ◆ What's happening with my body right now (e.g. posture, breathing etc.)?
> ◆ How would it be different if I were fully in touch with my power?
> Then simply change what you do with your body, to invite in the state of engagement and personal power.

The second mechanism for state change relates to the way you communicate with yourself. This forms the basis for all the bounce-back principles, as each involves communicating an insight to yourself as a way of helping you deal with falls and difficult times. For example, when you've flopped badly and are about to kick yourself, just remembering that phrase 'the way to succeed is to double your failure rate' can change the way you look at the situation.

A different conversation can occur in your mind. Instead of an inner commentary running you down, you can shift towards the kind of 'positive self-talk' that turns the situation around.

The way you feel about something depends on which aspects of it you focus your attention on. When you think of the bits of your life you're grateful for, you feel differently than when chewing over your dissatisfactions. Because your direction of gaze is steered by the questions you ask yourself, this leads to a simple and effective way of shifting your state. You ask yourself a question that powers you.

For example, asking 'What am I determined about?' focuses your attention in a way that strengthens determination. Developing good questions and asking yourself these regularly is such an easy thing to do, yet you may be surprised by what a difference it makes. Try it out and see.

> **Try this: Questions that power you**
> Think of three questions that can help change the state you're in, such as:
> ◆ What am I really happy about? What excites me? What am I grateful for?
> ◆ What do I feel strongly about? What am I determined about?
> Get into the habit of asking yourself these questions every day.

A question that leads into the next principle is: 'Who can I ask for support?'

I can't, we can

In the groups I run with my alcoholic clients, support from others is commonly mentioned as making a crucial difference in a crisis. Picking up the phone and having a conversation can be a life-saver. Yet even in crisis, there are often blocks in the way of asking for help. One of the biggest turning points is when people recognize that they can't solve their problems alone, and so reach out and ask for help.

A common block to seeking help is the idea that to be strong you need to sort things out yourself. This is a limiting belief, because it stops you finding the strength that is generated between people. This is *power with*. What's great about this collaborative view of power is that when people help each other, both sides benefit. The giver feels good about what they're doing, and the receiver gets the help they need. But there's something else too: the bonds of relationship grow. The following story about the difference between heaven and hell communicates something about the difference that giving and receiving support can make.

A group of people sit round a huge banqueting table covered with food. But they all have damaged elbows and this makes them unable to bend their arms. This means they can't pick up the food to feed themselves. Looking hungry and frustrated, these people are in hell.

In another room, an identical table is also laden with food. The folk here seem gloriously happy. They have discovered that their fixed extended arms are the perfect length for feeding other people. Not only do they have the joy of eating, but also of receiving from others and of giving too. This is heaven.

How many of your friendships have deepened during times when you've either given or received support? If everyone were self-sufficient, we wouldn't need to reach out to each other in the way that builds and strengthens nourishing relationships.

Trust in something larger than yourself

In order to develop your resources for dealing with crisis, it is useful to ask yourself: 'Where do I turn to for strength?' It might be your friends or family, a support group or mentor, it might even be a pet or a special place where you feel more at peace. I think of these sources of strength as similar to the roots of a plant. They anchor us.

When you look at a tree, it is amazing to think that there is a mirror image of growth below the ground, such that what you see is only half of the tree. During periods of drought, the roots extend. The barren times provoke the tree to connect more firmly with the ground out of which it grows. Something similar can happen for us. It is only when we really need help that we're likely to appreciate the importance of our root system. And our connections can extend beyond our immediate circle of friends or family to also include spiritual sources of strength.

Spirituality is to do with our feeling of connection with something beyond ourselves. It may involve a belief in God or membership of a religion, but it doesn't have to. It is more about having a sense that there is something bigger than your own life and that this can offer you both purpose and support.

In recent years there's been growing interest in the role of spiritual factors in helping people face the crisis of serious illness. In a research study on cardiac surgery patients, those who drew strength from their spirituality were three times more likely to survive their operation.[7] Another piece of research looked at women who had fractured a hip.[8] Those who identified spiritual sources of strength were less likely to become depressed and recovered their ability to walk more quickly.

Being able to draw strength from something larger than yourself lies at the heart of the approach of *power through*. At first this might seem a mysterious term, but as you will see, it can be looked at in both practical and spiritual ways. Because this perspective can make such a difference to your experience of personal power, and because it can lead to the deeper shifts that help you maintain stamina and endurance, the next section of the book describes in more detail how you can develop it.

Power Points

1 Whenever you mess up badly or disaster strikes, consider the possibility that this could become a turning point for the better. Bounce-back principles help you get up after the falls in a way that makes this more likely.

2 It's not whether you fail but how you respond when you do fail that makes the biggest difference to long-term success. Setbacks alert you to areas where adjustments are needed and this can help you make better decisions in the future. Hence the saying: 'The way to succeed is to double your failure rate.'

3 Even if you have a positive outlook, it can still hurt when things go wrong. Think of this as an emotional bruise. Feeling upset can be part of the grieving process that helps you adjust to a new reality. Be understanding with yourself as you take the time you need to get back on your feet.

4 Crisis sometimes brings out the best in us; when this happens we may feel strengthened by difficult circumstances and more alive during them. However, awful situations can also push people into states of shock, panic, defeat or denial. You can improve your ability to rise to the challenge of facing a crisis by learning how to move into engaged and resourceful states.

5 Blotting out problems might seem attractive because it offers instant relief from the stress of disturbing realities. However, when we ignore difficulties they mount up, becoming more difficult to face and leading to a vicious cycle. Any training to prepare yourself to deal with crisis needs to address both the temptations and the dangers of denial.

6 Your direction of gaze is steered by the questions you ask yourself. This leads to a simple and effective way of shifting your state: you ask yourself a question that powers you. For example, asking 'What am I determined about?' focuses your attention in a way that strengthens determination.

7 Like the roots of a tree, psychological, social and spiritual sources of strength can anchor you. By developing these, you increase your capacity to face and deal with difficult situations.

Part III

The Power to Keep Yourself Going

"If I had to select one quality, one personal characteristic that I regard as being most highly correlated with success, whatever the field, I would pick the trait of persistence. Determination. The will to endure to the end, to get knocked down seventy times and get up off the floor saying, "Here comes number seventy-one!"'
Richard M DeVos

9

Connected Vision

My friend Sandra had only been well a few weeks before she started to feel faint again. Her kidney infection had returned. This time it was worse than before and I got a call telling me she'd been admitted to hospital. As I prepared to go in and see her, I wondered what I could bring. Fruit, flowers and chocolate are the usual offerings on such occasions, but would they strengthen her ability to get well? I had an old personal stereo I wasn't using and I collected together some music and relaxation tapes to go with it. While this might boost my friend's morale, could it also aid her recovery from infection?

The view of conventional medicine is that each illness is caused by a specific defect. The role of the doctor is to hunt out the 'sick bit', to identify what the defect is and then, if possible, to put it right. Sandra was in the renal ward under the care of a specialist kidney team. Their focus was the infection in her kidney, which they treated with powerful intravenous antibiotics. From the perspective of this highly targeted approach, whether Sandra listened to tapes or not was irrelevant. However, this was her fourth kidney infection in less than a year. Each time antibiotics had worked for a while, but then she got sick again.

The issue facing Sandra and her doctors is one relevant to any type of change. Once you've made the initial shift, how do you keep things that way? Whether it is recovery from infection, giving up a habit or transforming an organization, the key to maintaining a change is to cultivate a context that supports it. This chapter describes how you can do this, introducing the essential tool of connected vision.

What is connected vision?

Connected vision is a way of looking at situations where you focus on the relationships between different aspects and on how these aspects act together as a whole. This is different from the more usual approach within science of splitting something into segments and then focusing on these one at a time.

The splitting approach is seen in most universities, where each department usually specializes in a different fragment of reality. Something similar occurs in hospitals, where for example the cardiology department attends to a person's heart and hepatology their liver. Focusing on the pieces, whether of people or our world, has led to spectacular advances in understanding. But it is an incomplete view. As the dots puzzle in Chapter 6 demonstrated, focusing too narrowly can create blocks to problem solving.

Connected vision opens up new ways forward because it brings into view features of reality that can't be seen with the narrow focus approach. You already do this quite naturally, as the following experiment shows.

> **Try this: The thumb experiment**
> ◆ Hold your hand at arm's length in front of your nose.
> ◆ Close one eye then look at your thumb.
> ◆ Swap eyes, so that you look through the other eye.
> ◆ Compare views. Are they the same or slightly different?
> ◆ Now look through both eyes. What happens?

When you look first through one eye and then the other, the thumb's relationship to its background changes. Each eye therefore sees a slightly different image. When you bring the two views together, something new emerges: depth.

The depth of three-dimensional vision is an example of an emergent property. This is something that isn't found in either of the parts themselves but only comes into being when they act together to form a larger whole. When you look through one eye the image is two dimensional. It is the way the image from each eye is combined with the other that leads to a three-dimensional view.

What we have here are two different ways of looking at reality: one that divides into parts, the other that joins into wholes. Focusing on the *parts* is called reductionism, because you're reducing something complex to its basic building blocks. Looking at things *as a whole* is called holism, the core assumption here being that the whole is more than the sum of the parts. The whole is more because it has emergent properties that the parts, by themselves, don't have.

It's not that one view is right and the other wrong. Rather, like having two eyes, when we integrate both approaches we get more depth of vision. This is because each view draws attention to a different aspect of what's going on. I think of this in terms of foreground and background.

Foreground and background

When we focus attention on something, this becomes the foreground. Anything else falls out of the spotlight into the distance of the background (see Figure 9.1). In deep concentration, that background may even seem to disappear altogether.

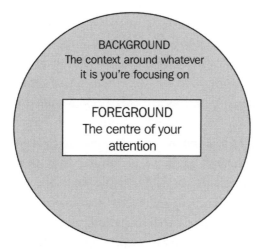

Figure 9.1 Foreground and background

When you see the world in terms of separate pieces, it may make sense to study them one at a time. You can give your full attention to each part without being distracted. Breaking a big project down into manageable chunks means that you can concentrate on one step before moving on to the next. However, if you only focus on what's in front of your nose, you miss seeing the bigger picture.

Connected vision starts from the assumption that any-thing you look at is always part of something larger. To understand what's happening in the foreground, you also need to look at the background context around it. This involves taking a step back and seeing things as a whole.

With the building block approach to medicine, illness is seen as all down to a faulty part. This perspective sug-gests that when you are ill, you need to see someone who knows about that part. The sick bit becomes the fore-ground, the focus of attention. This approach emphasizes the role of specialists; they're regarded as the ones who know what's what, and getting well is seen to depend on what they do.

However, the sick bit is only part of the story. Each dis-eased part exists in a larger context that includes the per-son as a whole as well as their social and physical environment. Considering this background gives you a wider view of both causes of illness and resources for recovery. This is the holistic approach to healthcare.

If health is thought of as similar to a boat moving through water, illness is when the boat hits a rock (see Figure 9.2).[1] Doctors and other health professionals are like geologists: they know lots about rocks and have vari-ous ways of dealing with them. These include powerful potions to dissolve them away and scalpels for their surgi-cal removal. Sometimes this can be life saving. But it is only one approach. The water level represents the effect of background factors, such as our resistance to disease. When we are run down or at a low ebb, this is reduced, and we're more likely to crash into the rocks of illness.

Just treating rocks and leaving the water level low puts the person at risk of soon crashing again. So when I worked as a GP I used to ask my patients: 'Why do you

Health is like travelling in a boat.

Illness is like crashing into a rock. When the water level is low, this is more likely to happen.

Figure 9.2 The rowing boat model

think this is happening now?' Whether they had headaches, asthma, depression or infections, they often identified recent stressful events that had triggered their illness. By recognizing factors that left them run down, they named areas they could address to help their recovery (such as attending to diet or stress).

Each of us has a powerful self-healing capacity that repairs injuries and resists disease. By looking at how we create contexts that support this, the holistic approach aims to strengthen our ability to heal ourselves. This is like raising the water level (see Figure 9.3).

Raising the water level means you don't crash into rocks so often.

Figure 9.3 Raising the water level

When the focus of medicine is on the sick bit, the rocks are the foreground; the background water level can easily get neglected. When my friend Sandra was in hospital, her doctors didn't pay much attention to what was happening in her life at the time. With the recent break-up of a long-term relationship, this had been one of the most stressful periods she'd ever had. Instead, with their gaze on the kidney, their response was to consider surgically removing the organ as a way of preventing further infections.

Talk of a possible operation pushed Sandra into a state of anxiety. As high levels of fear lead to release of stress hormones that reduce resistance to infection, a context was being created that made further infections more likely. This is why I brought in the relaxation tapes. The body has a relaxation response that is physiologically the opposite of the stress response. Relaxation exercises and certain types of music can trigger states of calm where the heart rate slows down and levels of stress hormones fall. This can help someone recharge in a way that allows their water level to rise.

What I like about the rowing boat metaphor is that it invites a both/and approach that addresses both the foreground and the background. While the expertise of professionals is valuable when dealing with rocks, raising the water level is something we can all do. This is a way of finding our power when facing health concerns; it also makes it more likely that we'll stay well once we've got over the rock.

You can apply this metaphor to many other areas of change. Relationships, for example, hit the rocks when they run into trouble. One approach to restoring harmony is to tackle the issue causing problems (focusing on the rock); another is to strengthen the background of the relationship (raising the water level). These approaches can help each other. When relationships improve, they can float over difficulties that easily become crash points when things aren't going so well.

So how do you raise the water level? How do you cultivate a context that supports the changes you want to make? A practical tool you can use to help you here is the force-field analysis.

A force-field analysis is a way of mapping out factors that influence a situation. This brings the various background forces together so that you can see the effects of a context as a whole. You can then identify points where your actions make a difference, giving you plenty of options for practical steps. You can use this when facing health problems, but it can also be used for any other type of change. Here's how it's done.

Using a force-field analysis

1 The first stage is to identify the change you want to make. I'm going to demonstrate how this process might help my friend Sandra respond to her kidney infection. The change she wants to make is to get well.

2 The second stage is to identify any background factors that have a positive influence on the change you want to make. It doesn't matter how small the effects are, just anything that might add to a context that makes your desired change more likely. Good sleep, feeling calm, healthy nutrition and feeling supported are all factors that might help Sandra get well. Represent these by drawing arrows pushing a line upwards (see Figure 9.4). The line represents the state of the current context. Anything that lifts the line raises the water level.

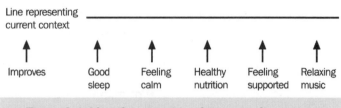

Figure 9.4 Identifying positive factors in the context

3   *The third stage is to identify any background factors that have a negative effect on the change you want to make. Again it doesn't matter how small they are, just anything that creates resistance or makes your desired change less likely. Feeling depressed, anxious, isolated and bored in hospital all add to a context that interferes with healing. Scarring from past kidney infections also makes future problems more likely. Represent any negative factors by drawing arrows pushing the line downwards.*

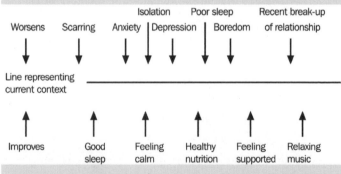

Figure 9.5 Identifying positive and negative factors in the context

4   *Looking at Sandra's arrows (Figure 9.5), at the moment it looks like there are more negative factors than positive ones. However, this is just the*

> starting point. Anything she can do to weaken the negative side or add to the positive will shift the context in a way that supports her desired change. The fourth stage is to identify practical steps you can take. Each time you do this, you open up personal power. For example, deciding to play an active part in getting well creates another positive factor. And each action based on this decision generates more arrows pushing the line upwards.
>
> 5 The fifth stage is to take the steps. And to keep taking them.

Will it make any difference?

When looking at the force-field analysis, you might find it hard to believe that some of the influences I've put down really make much difference. For example, will reducing boredom by listening to relaxation tapes really improve Sandra's chances of recovery?

It is well established that high stress levels can impair the body's resistance to infection.[2] There is also research evidence that self-help relaxation exercises can boost immune function by increasing the responsiveness of the white blood cells that fight infection.[3] But even though I tell you this, and list references at the back of the book, you may still doubt whether this is really effective. What needs to happen to convince you?

Having a scientific background, I value research studies. But if I use a treatment myself and find it incredibly helpful, then whatever the studies say, I'm going to have confidence in this approach. In a study looking at what convinced doctors a treatment was effective, personal experience was the highest-rated source of information.[4] Research papers came lower down the list. However, both personal experience and research studies tend to draw on the same principle of cause and effect. If a particular activity is reliably followed by certain consequences, then we generally think of the activity as causing these.

This way of looking at cause and effect creates problems for the context approach to change. When you exercise, meditate or turn down the offer of chocolate cake, you don't always experience an immediate benefit. Many of the steps to promote change at context level don't, by themselves, have a clear, measurable effect. It may not seem worth the effort. To see the benefits of background changes, you need to look in a different way. This is because they operate on a model of cause and effect that moves beyond the usual form of *A* causes *B*.

Two ways of looking at cause and effect	
Direct effect	A causes B
Indirect effect	A adds to a context that makes B more likely

The three circles of influence

I find it useful to think of three levels of influence, which I represent by three circles (Figure 9.6). The first is the circle of control, which refers to all the things you have direct control over. When something is under your control, you can predict what the results of your actions will be. For example, you can flick a switch and know that a light will come on. This is the *A* causes *B* model. Power is

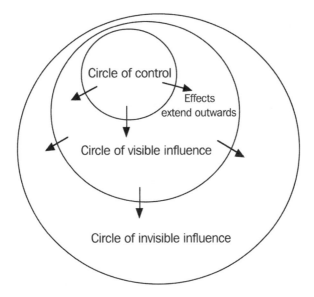

Figure 9.6 Three levels of influence

often thought of like this, being viewed as the ability to cause things to happen.

The second level is the circle of visible influence. This includes all the situations you can visibly affect, but don't directly control. For things in this circle you are *a* cause of what happens, rather than *the* cause. For example, you might decide you want to improve your relationship with a work colleague. The way you act towards them may visibly influence how they react to you, but you don't control them. They choose their own response, so you can't predict with certainty what the effects of your actions will be.

The third level is the circle of invisible influence. Here the effects of your actions are so small, delayed or distant that it is difficult to directly link them to what you do. Because this type of influence is hard to see, we often don't recognize it. Yet when you find ways of uncovering it, the range of your power expands.

Over two decades ago, I carried out some research on the use of biofeedback in relaxation training. Subjects had their heart rates monitored and were able to see this displayed on a computer screen. Our heart rate normally lies outside our conscious control, but it is something we can influence. You can get it to speed up by vigorous exercise; getting it to slow down from its normal resting rate is more difficult. Yet when people were able to see what their heart rate was doing, they were able to learn to slow it down more easily. They could see the effects of relaxation strategies, and were able to use this to guide them to methods that slowed the heart well.

Biofeedback makes visible an influence that is normally just outside our vision. When we can see the consequences of what we're doing, it is easier to see how our choices influence what happens. By learning to extend our vision, we open up personal power.

Learning to see the five mountains

If you want to lose weight or give up a habit like smoking, you'll often face situations where you feel tempted. An option presents itself that offers to take away your tension, provide pleasurable sensations or otherwise boost your day in a way you find attractive. You know from past experience that it works. *A* causes *B*; this option causes something you like. Why resist?

The words that often lead people to succumb are 'just one won't hurt'. There is a truth here, in that if you were to precisely calculate the effect of one cigarette, drink or chocolate bar, taken in isolation and not followed by others, the effect would be minuscule. This is the fragmented view of reality, where each thing is seen in its own little box, neatly separated from everything else. But when you look further, you see something different.

The key question with connected vision is: 'What's it part of?' If a cigarette, drink or chocolate bar contributes to your life in a way you're happy with, it's your life and your choice. But when it's part of a habit that's taking you somewhere you don't want to go, then you see temptation in a different way.

With connected vision you look beyond the moment. You recognize how small things can feed into and create something larger. The sixth-century Chinese poet Wang Ming saw this too when he wrote:

Water dripping ceaselessly
will fill the four seas;
specks of dust not wiped away
will become the five mountains.

The way you feel about something depends on which aspects of it you think about. If you bring one of your favourite pleasures to mind, you might smile and feel a glow, remembering times you've enjoyed it. When you associate an activity with pleasure, the idea that it might be bad for you can be an unwelcome one. Giving up or cutting down feels like a loss, like something being taken away from you. To be able to let go of something you enjoy, you need to find an even deeper desire to replace it with. This is finding the *want* behind the *should*.

Tim (see p 25) gave up smoking when he saw how it was blocking him from achieving the things he wanted most. It was a drain on his resources. He saw further than the moments after meals he had so enjoyed with tobacco. He had a positive vision to head for and smoking was in the way. Temptation was just a question asking him what he really wanted. With each cigarette he refused, he gave his vote.

Layers of context

So far, what we've been looking at is how viewing something in isolation gives you a limited view. Whether it's a diseased organ or a single cigarette, whatever you look at is always part of something larger. This is also true of ourselves. Each of us is one small part of a larger world.

Treating a kidney but ignoring the person is similar to treating individuals but not considering the world they live in. The relationship in both cases is between smaller part and larger whole. This association between parts and wholes can be seen at many levels: a cell is a collection of molecules; an organ is made of smaller cells; a person comprises many organs; each person is a smaller part of a larger family, community, society and so on (see Figure 9.7). Rather than seeing our world as separate fragments, this way of looking sees interconnected layers where influence travels in both directions. We are affected by our cells and by our society; what we do influences them too.

Just as disease in organs is more likely when the general condition of a person is weakened, so illness in individuals is more likely when the condition of our world deteriorates. When someone gets cancer, Parkinson's disease or dementia, it is often thought of as bad luck. Yet looking at western society as a whole, these illnesses are becoming more common. This may be partly explained by people living longer, but there is also evidence linking these conditions with rising pollution levels.[5]

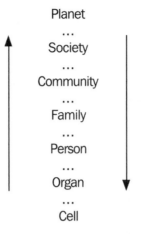

Planet
...
Society
...
Community
...
Family
...
Person
...
Organ
...
Cell

Figure 9.7 Influence goes both up and down

The fumes coming out of factory chimneys and car exhausts are like smoking on a collective basis. In the short term we experience the benefits and convenience of a highly industrialized society; it is only when we stand back and view a bigger picture that we see the problems. There are now over 77,000 chemicals in widespread use, many of these only invented in recent decades.[6] Most of them have not had proper safety checks. Pesticide residues have been found in breast milk, the blood of newborn babies, even in penguins in the Arctic. They are everywhere.

One in three people in Europe and North America will get cancer, and rates continue to rise. Dementia has become three times as common in the last 20 years.[7] In all, over 180 medical conditions have been linked to environmental pollution.[8] While human-made chemicals are not the only cause of many of these illnesses, they are a contributing factor. The toxic contamination of our food, air and water supplies creates a context that makes it more likely we will get sick.

Turning things around

The first stage of change is awareness. But even when we know about an issue, there are still obstacles in the way of being able to respond to it. As with any area of change, two key areas are motivation (does it bother us?) and capacity (could we make any difference even if we wanted to?).

The principles for motivating change with environmental issues are similar to those involved in losing weight or giving up smoking. First, we need to see good reasons for doing something; secondly, those reasons need to outweigh the motives for doing nothing or even for resisting change. The problem is that many polluting activities have benefits that seem immediate and clear, while the costs might be viewed as long term and distant. Spraying a garden with chemicals, flying to exotic locations, relying on a car even for short journeys – all of these can seem so convenient. To see the costs, we need to extend our range of vision (see Figure 9.8).

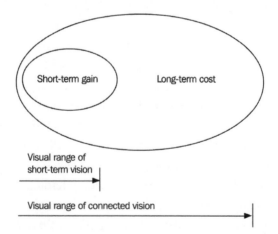

Figure 9.8 Short-term vision misses the long-term costs

In 1989, the *Exxon Valdez* oil tanker crashed into rocks, spilling its contents and covering over 1000 miles of Alaska's shoreline with oil. An unlucky disaster? Perhaps. Yet according to Greg Pallast,[9] the investigator hired by the Chugach tribal people who live in the region, there had been a series of cover-ups and short cuts on safety in the years leading up to the disaster. Four years earlier, managers at nearby Valdez port had been warned that there was insufficient equipment and staff to contain a medium or large oil spill. Just ten months before the spill, a top-level meeting of oil company executives in Arizona had been warned that safety equipment was inadequate. And on board the tanker itself, the radar had been switched off because it wasn't working properly. It had been broken for a year but not repaired.

Many other chemical spills, like the Bhopal disaster in India, have a similar history of cost cutting on safety measures. Why such recklessness? The short answer: avoiding spills is often seen as less important than maximizing profits. With short-term vision, theoretical risk is less compelling than money in the bank.

Seeing your power to change things

So how is connected vision helpful here? It enables you to see the links that give you reasons, and therefore motivation, to address an issue. When you are in a good state, you are in a stronger position to tackle an issue. Personal power is therefore helped by a context of wellness in your life. With connected vision you see how your personal wellbeing is influenced by the state of the world around you. The personal and the planetary become intimately linked.

But are you able to make any difference to the environment around you? If you see yourself as separate from the world, it may be difficult to believe you can change it. Connected vision, on the other hand, recognizes the power of context. You are part of the context for everything else that happens. Your actions, even your thoughts and ways of looking, all contribute to the background that influences any issue that concerns you.

Although your actions may only have tiny effects on the grand scheme of things, each one functions as a vote that feeds movement in a particular direction. I think of this as a holistic democracy, where you're voting with all of your choices, rather than just with one small cross on a piece of paper every few years. Because you have many such votes every day, this perspective expands your circle of influence. If you're concerned about chemicals, your shopping choices can vote for an agriculture that doesn't use pesticides. It is easy to blame oil company executives who put profit before pollution control, but if you have savings in accounts that aren't ethically screened, you may, unwittingly, be doing the same thing.[10] By looking at the invisible influence of any money you have saved, you give yourself added voting power.

One choice by itself may not make much difference, but with connected vision you see that each action is always part of something larger. The little choices used to be discounted. But more and more we are recognizing that our actions have ripples extending far beyond what we can see.

Power Points

1 We are usually taught to tackle issues by making them the focus of our attention. Another approach is to step back and look at how you can influence the background context around the issue. These two approaches work best when combined.

2 If you've been unsuccessful with more direct methods, cultivating a context that supports your desired change can tip the balance in your favour. Because of this, addressing background factors can open up new ways of moving forward when you're feeling blocked.

3 The context approach is also useful when you want to maintain a change you've already made, such as to keep to a decision. This can help you reinforce determination, prevent relapses and boost confidence.

4 Some background factors seem to have little effect when looked at in isolation. Because of this they are often dismissed as being insignificant. It is only when you see how they act together as part of a larger context that you appreciate their power. This is where connected vision is important: it is a way of looking that helps you recognize how small parts can play important roles in a bigger picture. This helps you find your power.

5 With connected vision, you don't look at things in isolation. Rather, you look at the relationships between different areas and at how various aspects of a situation act together as a larger whole. A question that invites this approach is:

'What's it part of?' When looking this way, small steps become seen as part of larger journeys, and seemingly isolated incidents become recognized as part of larger patterns.

6 A force-field analysis is a way of mapping out factors that influence a situation. This brings the various background forces together so that you can see the effects of a context as a whole. You can then identify points where your choices make a difference, providing plenty of options for action.

10

Believing Mirrors

*I*recently saw an ex-client who had been sober for many years. I asked her what had helped her get well. 'I felt believed in,' she said. Although she hadn't initially had much confidence in herself, she felt that those working with her at our unit had believed that she could recover from her alcoholism. This challenged her old thinking, which expected her to fail at everything. What she had found useful was having a 'believing mirror', a term coined by Julia Cameron in her book *The Artist's Way*.[1] Here is how she describes it:

> Put simply, a believing mirror is a friend to your creativity and someone who believes in you and your creativity.

Among the most important parts of our context are the people around us and, when they reflect back a positive belief in our ability and potential, this strengthens our confidence in ourselves. This fuels a self-amplifying loop in a way that generates a self-fulfilling prophecy (see Figure 10.1). In this chapter we look at how you can develop and strengthen a network of support around you. When you have this, it can encourage and sustain you in a way that helps keep you going.

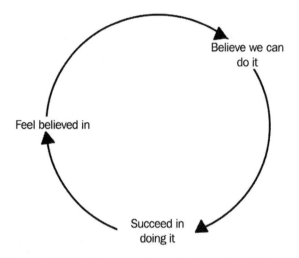

Figure 10.1 Believing mirrors fuel a self-fulfilling prophecy

The roots of self-belief

If you believe that you're unable to do something, you're unlikely even to attempt it. If you do have a go, you're less likely to persevere once you hit difficulty. Since belief is such an important factor in finding your power, it is worth pausing for a moment and asking: 'Where does belief come from?'

Self-help writer Anthony Robbins defines belief as a feeling of certainty about something.[2] Like a table held up by its legs (Figure 10.2), he points out that each belief needs to be supported by reference points or evidence. For example, I have a belief that I can sing and have many memories of musical occasions to back this up. These references give me a feeling of certainty about my ability. When there is an opportunity to sing, I jump into it with relish and so develop more reference memories to support my belief. But I think of my friend Betty (see p 125),

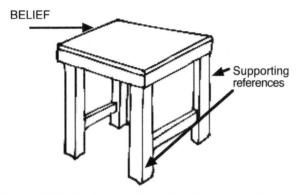

Figure 10.2 Each belief is held up by supporting reference information

who as a child was told to 'mouth it' so that she moved her lips without making a sound. For decades, this was a reference that propped up the belief that she couldn't sing. When people sung around her, she kept quiet and so collected more reference memories to hold up the belief that she wasn't a singer.

If you've succeeded at doing something in the past, then you've got something to support the belief that you can do it again. But how do you get to believe you can do something you've never done before?

Reference groups

As well as looking at our own experience, we also base our beliefs on what others around us say or do. If I've never put up shelves, for example, but I know that plenty of my friends have, then it is easier to believe this is possible for me too. My thinking is that if they can do it, I probably can too. My friends in this case become my reference group: the points of reference I use to judge whether I can do something or not. My reference group might also extend to include people I've read about or seen on television if something they've said or done influences my beliefs about what's possible for me.

Our reference group also gives us messages about ourselves. These are so important in the development of our identity and self-beliefs that the American psychologist Charles Horton Cooley[3] coined the term the 'looking glass self'. He suggested that our sense of who we are grows out of noticing other people's reactions to us. For example, if a child hears someone describe them as intelligent, this creates a reference supporting the self-belief 'I am intelligent'.

The family we grow up in becomes our first reference group, and many of our deep-seated beliefs about ourselves have their origins in comments that family members made about us when we were young. However, self-belief is not something set in childhood and then fixed. You can change and influence it by becoming more aware of what reference groups you are using and choosing to change these if they are giving you undermining messages.

When Robbie was a child she had hearing problems. This made it difficult for her to develop language, so she didn't speak properly. When she tried to express herself, her dad would tell her to stop speaking rubbish. She grew up being told she was stupid and she believed it.

Self-beliefs like this become self-fulfilling prophecies, and in Robbie's case she gave up trying because she expected herself to fail. She left school early and ended up becoming an alcoholic. It was many years later, in treatment, that she began to realize how the messages she received as a child had contributed to her belief that she was a failure. When I interviewed her, she told me: 'I always carried around my dad's mould of what he wanted me to be, but I could never live up to it, so I felt a failure.'

One of the most significant turning points for Robbie was getting involved in the self-help group Alcoholics Anonymous. This provided a different reference group. She saw examples of people turning their lives around in a way that encouraged her to think that this might be possible for her. 'If they can do it, then perhaps I can too,' she thought. As she got to know other members of the group, trust and support grew. Being surrounded by people who believed in her ability to change her life for the better, she began to believe this too. Her drinking became a thing of the past.

In her 40s, Robbie started having driving lessons. She had never bothered before because she'd assumed she wouldn't succeed. But with new-found confidence, she passed first time. The positive wheel began to roll, each step forward giving her more confidence to carry on. She began to believe in herself.

Toxic reference groups

I think of believing mirrors as similar to the effect of sunlight on plants: they nourish and stimulate growth. However, just as toxins in soil can cause plants to wither, so too can destructively critical put-downs stunt the growth of confidence. This was what happened to Robbie in childhood. One of the ways to notice such negative effects is to check how you feel when you talk in the presence of others. Do you feel encouraged or undermined?

The signals may be subtle, but if there is a consistent sagging in your self-esteem every time you are in the company of a particular person or group, you may need to review whether you want them as part of your reference group. One of the people I interviewed told me how she had done this:

> I felt there were people around me that weren't in support of me. I felt judged by them, as though I was constantly doing things wrong in their eyes. It reached the stage where I didn't want to be around them any more. So I got a new address book and only included in it the people I wanted to keep in touch with. I feel relief to have moved on. Now I'm with a different set of people, life has become so much better.

She found her power to create a positive context around her.

Cultivate support around you

There is likely to be part of you that believes in your ability, but perhaps also an inner cynical voice that doesn't. If you're surrounded by cynical people (see Figure 10.3), that side of you has plenty of reinforcements while your self-believing part is outnumbered. You can strengthen self-belief by consciously seeking out the people who you feel believe in you and recruiting them into your support network.

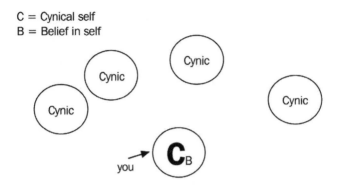

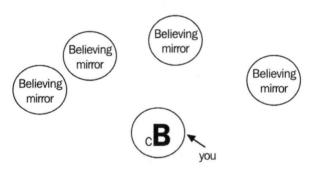

Figure 10.3 Creating a context of support

Identifying your support network

When you have an idea of something you'd like to take forward, who do you talk to? Our visions can grow through
telling others about them. Even if you feel discouraged by
others, think of them as threshold guardians who challenge
you to find ways through the problems they identify.
However, just as you protect young seedlings from hostile
weather, when your plans are still germinating, save them
for the people you'll get more encouraging support from.

When you find yourself talking excitedly with a spark in your eye, then you know you're on to something. Are there some people in your life you're more likely to have these kind of conversations with? If so, these are people you want in your support network.

When I use the term support network, I'm referring to the range of people you feel supported by. It is useful to reflect on who these are because they are valuable resources in your life. You want to treasure them. You may be part of their support network too; mutual support arrangements are stronger than one-way flows.

> ### Try this: Mapping your support network
> ◆ *Write your name in the centre of a sheet of paper.*
> ◆ *Around your name, write down all the people you feel supported by, and draw an arrow from each name to yours. The more support you get from them, the thicker the arrow you draw.*
> ◆ *Write down the names of the people you play an active role in supporting. Have an arrow from your name to theirs, and the more support you give, the thicker the arrow.*
> ◆ *Who are the believing mirrors? These are the people who reflect a positive belief in you and what you do. Put a circle by their name.*
> ◆ *Looking at your network as a whole, how do you feel? Are there any changes you'd like to make? Are there some relationships you'd like to strengthen, perhaps others you'd like to back away from?*

Figure 10.4 is an example of what a support network map might look like.

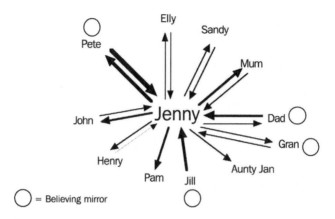

Figure 10.4 Example of support network map

The value of this type of mapping is that it shows you where your support is and isn't. In the example it became clear to Jenny that Jill was a valuable friend whom she felt supported by, but whom she'd been neglecting recently. This was partly because she'd been spending time with John helping him through a difficult time. It also became clear that John, Henry and Pam were not the best people to talk with about her hopes or plans for the future. She didn't feel the support of their belief in her.

If you do a support network map and don't identify anyone as a believing mirror, is this something you'd like to develop? How can you do this? It may be a case of strengthening the friendships that come closest, or actively seeking out new friends. If you don't have people who share your interests, values or concerns, how could you find some? The problem-solving process may help (see p 130).

1 + 1 = 2 and a bit

One of the biggest shifts in personal power comes when someone breaks out of the idea that they have to do everything by themselves. When you start involving other people in what you do, you open up the potential for synergy. This is where the combined effects of people working together lead to new or enhanced capabilities compared with what would happen if they were by themselves.

Research has compared the singing of mothers when their baby is in the room with the singing of mothers alone. When recordings of the same songs were played back to babies, they could tell the difference. They showed more interest in the songs sung in company. I notice something similar when I'm giving a talk. If I practise alone in a room, it isn't nearly as engaging as when I'm with people. As soon as other people are around, we enter a relationship that can draw out a different side of us. This 'evoking effect' is a good example of synergy: when it draws out our best qualities and performances, it can enhance our abilities.

When two people have this effect on each other, a creative spark can develop that stimulates the flow of new ideas. Such mutual inspiration is the basis for many great double acts, and is an example of *power with*. This is a different type of power: it isn't found in one person or the other, but grows out of the relationship between them.

With synergy, a new type of mathematics occurs, expressed by the equation $1 + 1 = 2$ and a bit. The 'and a bit' refers to the new properties or abilities that can emerge when people interact. A musical example of this is harmony: when people sing together, harmonies can be created. But if you listen to people individually one after the other, the harmonies aren't there. They only come into being when parts act together to make a larger whole.

You may be aware of times when people acting together achieve less than they would if they were by themselves. Synergy doesn't always happen, and sometimes one plus one can equal less than two. What makes the difference between relationships that enhance our lives and those that diminish them? What makes a partnership, friendship or team a good one? These are central questions for developing power with, and the ability to improve relationships is an essential skill in building effective support networks.

Some people appear to be naturally good at getting along with others, in a way that can make this seem like an innate ability. But increasingly, psychologists are recognizing that such interpersonal intelligence is based on learnable skills. Harvard psychologist Howard Gardner[4] writes:

Interpersonal intelligence is the ability to understand other people: what motivates them, how they work, how to work co-operatively with them.

To learn any skill, one of the first steps is simply to recognize that the area is important enough to give your attention to. If you want to learn a new skill or brush up on an old one, you give it time. You can develop power with by giving attention to what it is that builds and deepens harmony with other people. When you do this, more of your relationships become ones where 1 + 1 = 2 and a bit.

If you feed plants, water them and give them your attention, they grow. It is the same with relationships. When the space between people gets neglected, like the water level falling (see Figure 10.5), this creates a context where the relationship is more prone to crashes.

Figure 10.5 A relationship hitting the rocks

Try this: Feeding your relationships

Think of a relationship you would like to improve. Use the dream cycle to:

◆ *Review how things are at the moment. What works, what doesn't, what are the issues, what are the strengths?*

◆ *Dream how you would like the relationship to be. Imagine that it has improved. How does that feel? What is different?*

◆ *Plan by identifying what would help the relationship. Identify practical steps you can take to give the connection a boost.*

◆ *Do – go and take the steps.*

◆ *Review – what went well, what didn't? How can you learn from this? What do you still need to find out about? Continue round the cycle again.*

Creating support structures

Many people have blocks about asking for help. These include the fear of burdening others and also the fear of conflict. When I explore these fears on courses I run, I ask people how they feel when others ask them for help. They often feel pleased, some even say they feel honoured. Asking someone for help is a way of expressing your belief in them, as you are only likely to ask those you believe will be effective in helping you. People tend to feel valued by this. They will only feel burdened if, when it doesn't suit them to help, they have difficulties in saying no. You can reduce the risk of this by making it easy for them to decline your request if that is what they'd prefer to do. When you make it clear that it is fine for somebody to say no, it makes it easier for you to ask in the first place.

While informal support with friends and family can play a hugely important role, you can strengthen your network by setting up some kind of support structure. By structure I mean a collection of agreements and shared understandings that make clear what the support role is, and what might be expected in terms of when and how to meet. This may sound a bit formal, but what it does is empower people to play a more active support role than just casually chatting with you from time to time. This can also create opportunities for regular contact with people who are believing mirrors for you. Here are three examples of how this can work.

Asking someone to be your support person

I was running a course recently and I found out a week beforehand that the group was going to be larger than I'd expected. I knew that a friend was keen to do the course, but it was fully booked. So I asked him if he'd be willing to be my support person. That way I knew that there was someone I could count on for help if needed, and he got to do the course for free.

If you are going to do anything that is scary or challenging, inviting someone along as your support person can change the context in your favour. You know even before you start that there will be an ally there. Why would they want to do this? Supporting someone can be enjoyable, deepen friendships and be a way of learning from each other. It also means that the supporter feels part of a project without the stress of playing the central role. If you make clear what the role involves and make it easy for the other person to turn you down if they're not interested, it is their choice whether they come along with you or not.

Mutual support agreements

Co-counselling is a self-help approach based on giving and receiving attention. Two people meet and first one listens and gives attention to the other, who does most of the talking. After an agreed time (often about 30 minutes) they swap over. This principle of equal time each way can be used in many situations and doesn't have to involve counselling. Two friends might arrange to have a weekly check-in where they have 10 minutes each way by phone. I have friends who meet regularly to give attention to each other's gardens. Working together is more fun and often gets more done.

Support groups

Whenever you have a number of people gathered around a shared intention, you have a group. A support group is where that shared intention is to support each other. There are many ways of doing this. A feature that makes a group like this work well is having a mechanism for periodically checking whether participants find it helpful, so that changes can be made when it isn't.

One of the functions of being in a support role is to give supportive rather than destructive feedback. It is worth looking at how to do this.

Principles of constructive feedback

Being a believing mirror isn't about applauding everything someone does. If they make a mistake and don't realize this, they are likely to continue making the same error. In order to learn and improve, we all need help in identifying where we're getting it right and where we get it wrong.

Here are five principles that can be used to give supportive and constructive feedback.

Start with the positives

If the first comment someone hears is criticism, this can trigger an emotional reaction that makes it difficult to hear anything else. Defensiveness blocks learning. Start by saying what impressed you, what you liked and what you saw that worked well. In learning it is just as important to recognize what we're doing right as it is to see where we get it wrong. For example, someone may do something spectacularly badly, but you might still be impressed by their boldness for trying. If that's the case, don't hold back – tell them.

Always speak the truth

If you can't see anything that impresses you then look harder. Don't make something up. Insincere feedback discredits you as a reliable source of information.

Use process thinking

When you act as a believing mirror, you don't just see someone as they are, but also as they could be. To support someone to grow into the best they could be, you need to believe that this is possible. Process thinking helps, as you don't judge people merely on how they've been or how they are. Imagination is necessary to consider how someone could be if surrounded by encouraging, supportive influences. Then ask yourself how you could become one of these influences.

There are different ways of being right

Just because someone does something differently to how you'd do it, this doesn't mean they've got it wrong. Wait and see how it turns out. If it turns out badly, they might be interested in hearing about alternative strategies.

Be specific

In order to learn from feedback it needs to be specific. For example, a phrase like 'You're no good' just labels someone as useless. But if you tell them exactly what they've done that you think is no good, then they are in a better position to change it. The evaluation here is about a specific behaviour rather than about the person as a whole.

A simple way of expressing this is first stating your observation ('When you...') and then saying what your experience was when this happened ('I felt...'). This is an assertiveness technique that can also be used to challenge put-downs. Here's an example: 'When you repeatedly make jokes about me, I feel humiliated.' But this approach can also be used to give feedback about the things you're impressed by. For example, 'When you gave your presentation, I really liked the way you linked theory to practical examples.'

As a believing mirror you believe in someone's positive potential so much that you want to be an ally in helping them move towards that. Giving honest, specific feedback is one of the ways you can do this.

Changing group culture

The model of supportive and encouraging feedback I've described may seem far removed from what many people experience. How can you change the ethos of the family, social or work group you belong to if it is dominated by a culture of put-downs and cynicism?

One of the keys shifts in thinking in finding your power is from 'they should' to 'I will'. This involves recognizing the way you participate in the context you are part of. A simple step, like refusing to undermine anyone around you, can have a profound effect on the culture you belong to. Each time you give encouragement and support to others, you are voting for a social culture that supports and encourages. Each time you undermine someone else, you are taking part in, and therefore supporting, a culture that undermines people.

Styles of interaction are contagious, as we are all influenced by the way others communicate with us. If someone smiles at us, we are more likely to smile at the next person. Bad moods can also spread round groups of people just as a virus infection can. The difference is that with group culture or mood, we can choose what we pass on. And what we spread is likely to come bouncing back in our direction, as the following (anonymous) words express:

> *The way to be respected is to respect.*
> *The way to be trusted is to trust.*
> *The way to be liked is to like.*
> *The way to be loved is to love.*
> *What goes round comes around*
> *even if not straight away.*
> *What we put out to the world*
> *we breathe back in.*

The believing mirror principle involves recognizing how powerful the context around us is. When we have people around us who believe in and support us, like sunshine on plants, we grow. And the best way to develop believing mirrors in your life is to become one.

Power Points

1 Finding your power is strongly related to your beliefs about what is possible. These beliefs are based on reference points from own experience and from other people. You can boost your self-belief by identifying positive reference points.

2 Believing mirrors are people who reflect back belief in your potential. As positive reference points, they can help you create a self-fulfilling prophecy.

3 When those around you are undermining or reflect back disbelief, this can have a toxic effect, inhibiting your growth and potential.

4 By choosing to move away from undermining reference groups and increasing contact with people who act as believing mirrors for you, you cultivate a context that helps you grow in personal power and ability.

5 You can strengthen your support network by recruiting people into support roles or setting up mutual support agreements. This creates a structure that ensures a continuing supply of positive references to support your self-belief.

6 The evoking effect is where relationships draw out qualities or abilities not found when you are by yourself. This is an example of synergy, where the people acting together achieve more than they could individually. Mutual enhancement like this is the basis of all good double acts and teams.

7 Learning how to generate synergy is a key skill for developing power with. This is the type of power found not within people, but between them. It arises out of their relationships.

8 We can improve our relationships by giving them our attention. When we see them as important, we are more likely to feed them in a way that helps them grow.

11

The Power of Deeper Purpose

Victor Frankl,[1] psychiatrist and Auschwitz survivor, sometimes used to ask his patients: 'Why do you not commit suicide?' While a supportive context and believing mirror friends are great aids to determination, this question points you to something perhaps more powerful – your purpose and reasons for living. This chapter looks at how you find, or strengthen, the sort of inspiring purposes that keep you going, even through times of great difficulty. We also explore how such purposes can lead to more fulfilling lives, deepened personal power and constructive responses to global issues.

How to have a fulfilling life

In recent years there has been a growing interest in the scientific study of happiness and the factors that help create it. In his book *Authentic Happiness*, Martin Seligman[2] describes this positive psychology approach and summarizes its findings. He identifies three main approaches to improving life satisfaction and uses the terms 'pleasant life', 'engaged life'[3] and 'meaningful life' to describe these.

You can cultivate the pleasant life by learning to increase the strength and duration of pleasurable experiences. A simple example of this is savouring food. By chewing more slowly and giving your full attention to what you eat, you notice tastes and textures in a way that makes eating more enjoyable. You can apply this same principle of savouring to perception and memories too: when you notice something beautiful, or recall a past good time, don't rush on to the next thing. Chew it over in your mind and heart. In allowing your attention to settle for a moment in the places you feel grateful, you give your mood a boost.

Bursts of pleasure do feel good. The problem, though, is that the effects wear off quickly. If you repeat an enjoyable activity too often, you get used to it and it loses its appeal. Something similar happens with increased levels of wealth. As people adjust to improved circumstances, they get used to them. A continuing supply of more and better things may be needed to maintain satisfaction. That's why earning more money, once basic needs are met, usually makes little difference to long-term contentment. Studies[4] show happiness returning to previous levels within three months of a significant pay increase. To find deeper and more lasting fulfilment, an engaged and meaningful life is needed.

The engaged life involves developing flow activities, where you're so involved in what you do that time passes quickly. You feel this most when you're acting from your strengths in facing challenges that stretch you. You might be so absorbed that you don't notice how you're feeling at the time, but you're left with a warm glow afterwards. Many sports, hobbies and engaging occupations have this quality. By identifying your strengths and acting from them each day, you engage more in the flow states that add to quality of life.

244 The Power of Deeper Purpose

However, even the engaged life only goes so far. There may come a point where you stop and wonder what it is all for. A meaningful life is based on the longer-lasting satisfactions that come from acting for something larger than yourself. When you make a contribution to a community you value or serve a cause important to you, you experience a boost on a deeper level. This is the kind of satisfaction that leaves you feeling good about your life. It comes from recognizing ways you add value to our world and from seeing that your life has some meaning

In one of Seligman's psychology classes,[5] his students wondered whether happiness came more from meaningful acts or from having fun. To find out, he set them an assignment: before the next class, they were to perform one pleasurable activity and also one good deed, then write about them both. Many of the students were astonished by the results. Although the pleasurable things were fun while they lasted, acts of kindness left an afterglow of gratification. For some people this improved not just their day, but also the way they felt about themselves.

Recent research[6] has had similar findings. People were beeped several times a day; each time, they recorded what they were doing and how much they were enjoying themselves. When engaged in activities that developed their potential or contributed to others, they had higher levels of satisfaction than if they were doing something only for pleasure or relaxation.

These results are deeply significant because they question the either/or distinction sometimes made between self-interest and altruism. They suggest that if you want a truly fulfilling life, you need to find a purpose that goes deeper than merely meeting your own needs. I use the term 'deeper purpose' to refer to aims that serve something larger than you are. This is not only a source of heightened satisfaction in life. It also plays an important role in the development of personal power.

Four stages of development

Mihaly Csikszentmilhalyi, a world expert on happiness research, has developed a four-stage model of human development that weaves together both self-interest and the serving of deeper purposes.[7] In the first stage, the focus of concern is individual survival. Nourishment, shelter and protection from attack are the primary considerations. But once these basic needs are met, then the person expands their horizon to embrace the values of their community. The main concern becomes the wellbeing of their family, the neighbourhood where they live, or the social, religious or ethnic group they identify with. Nationalism is an extension of this second stage.

While the first stage is about *I* and *me*, the second stage is more about *us* and *we*. However, once someone is reasonably satisfied that their family, group or country is safe, then with the third stage the pendulum swings back to the individual. Personal fulfilment, finding yourself and the development of individuality become the principal concerns. There is a move away from blindly conforming to social pressures, accompanied by greater willingness to seek out and express personal truth.

The fourth stage, which builds on the previous three, involves an integration of personal and collective needs. In this, someone finds a way of serving their community through the expression of their individuality. In developing their gifts and purpose, they play a role that is uniquely theirs and that benefits others too.

Each of the four stages of development involves a different myth about who we are and what our purpose is. By myth I mean the story we see our lives as expressing. Psychotherapists David Feinstein and Stanley Krippner[8] put it like this:

> *Your myths address the broad concerns of identity (Who am I?), direction (Where am I going?) and purpose (Why am I going there?).*

In the first stage, life is seen as a competitive struggle and purpose viewed in an individualistic, 'grabbing for yourself' kind of way. When people are in fear, they may regress to this state and, as a result, see others around them as potential threats. In Figure 11.1, this is like seeing yourself as a separate square and viewing other squares with suspicion.

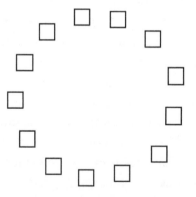

Figure 11.1 Are we separate, connected or both?

We are not well equipped to survive alone. That is why we evolved as social creatures who band together in groups. Charles Darwin recognized this when, in his book *The Descent of Man*,[9] he wrote: 'Selfish and contentious people will not cohere, and without coherence nothing can be effected.'

Darwin saw our tendency to care about each other as one of the things that gives us survival advantage. An individual human is no match for a sabre-toothed tiger, but as a coherent group we have added strength. For much of human history, purpose has been about survival of the group, and the heroes of many cultures have been those who protected the community from threat.

When someone strongly identifies with a group, it becomes part of who they are. Personal and collective wellbeing are seen as intimately bound; a threat to the group is experienced as an attack on the self. With this way of looking, identity is less to do with being a separate square and more about being a connected part of a larger circle (see Figure 11.1 again). Shared identity leads to feelings of closeness and loyalty to neighbouring squares. They are seen as part of the same larger self as you.

Having a strong connection with a group, such as a family or community, meets many personal needs. It gives you a feeling of belonging. It anchors you. If you need help there's some close by, and when others need help it feels natural to give it. But groups also have expectations and codes of behaviour; sometimes these can feel restrictive. What happens when there's something you want to do, but your group doesn't approve?

The rise of individual freedom is often seen as one of the great advances of modern societies. Rather than being tied down by tradition or community obligations, the door is opened to following your dreams. This is the third stage; personal power plays a central role in this, helping people find their truth and express themselves as empowered individuals. This may involve breaking free from old ways of being when these clash with personal liberty.

The downside of individualism is that, in shedding old stories of connectedness, it can leave people without a clear plot. The roles and responsibilities of being part of a community provide plenty of purpose. But when you shift focus away from the circle and back to the square, you can wonder what it is all for.

This change in storyline from *us* to *me* is happening in many parts of our world; increasingly, communities are losing coherence and competition between individuals is becoming seen as the natural order of things. When people lose their sense of belonging, a culture of selfishness emerges. Margaret Thatcher's famous statement[10] 'There's no such thing as society' applied to Figure 11.1 would be like saying 'There's no such thing as a circle, only squares'.

If we don't have a larger story to give meaning to our lives, purpose can become reduced to chasing pleasures, accumulating possessions or acquiring status. In the rat race this leads to, the value of things becomes measured by how much they help you get ahead. The big question here is whether this 'ahead' is somewhere you really want to get to. Self-help author Stephen Covey[11] writes:

> It's incredibly easy to get caught up in an activity trap, in the busy-ness of life, to work harder and harder at climbing the ladder of success only to discover it's leaning against the wrong wall.

By pausing to look at the plot of your life, you can check how much the purposes you're following are ones you feel fully engaged with.

Try this: Clarifying purpose
♦ *Complete the following open-ended sentence: 'What's really important to me is... because...'*
♦ *Keep repeating this; see if you can fill a page.*
♦ *Identify the five purposes that matter to you most.*

Being part of a larger story

Your life becomes meaningful when what it serves is important to you. But with the move from the third stage of development to the fourth, there is a shift in the plot. Rather than just focusing on personal advancement, a balance is found between meeting your own needs and contributing to the circles you are part of. With this, you bring together two sides of yourself: a connected self that belongs to larger circles and a separate self of the individual square. Integrating these two leads to a synergy that enhances personal power.

With your separate self, you develop your sense of personal authority. This combines trust in your inner sense of truth with the courage to live by it. When you follow your truth, you discover and develop the strengths that are uniquely yours. From your connected self, you experience passion, belonging, meaning, love and spirituality. These not only add to your aliveness, they also give you something to live for. Your connected self places you within a larger framework of meaning; it is from this bigger picture that deeper purposes flow.

In a hundred years' time, the grandchildren of today's children will be having their day. When their lives matter to you, when you feel part of the same extended family or community as them, you inhabit a story that spans a wider time frame than that of your own life. But it is easy to become overwhelmed by the challenges this story presents you with. Many people I interviewed felt so hopeless about the future that they didn't want to look at it. Global warming, rising toxin levels, resource depletion, international violence and other threats all add together to a present a gloomy picture. How can you find your power to face and respond to this?

Taking one potential threat as an example, I offer six principles that help open up your power when facing such concerns. I'll also show how rising to these 'bigger picture' challenges can help us find new strengths, taking our experience of personal power to a new level.

See your life as an adventure story

Many great adventure stories are based on the same general plot: a community faces a threat to its survival and the story is of how the main characters respond. Sometimes the danger is introduced in the opening scenes. Other times it is hidden at the start, revealing itself slowly. Either way, a common feature is that the threat, once recognized, initially seems overwhelming. But what makes these stories worth telling is that the central characters are not put off. They rise to the challenge.

The ingredients of a great story are not far different from the ingredients of a great life. You need a plot that engages you, where you can play a meaningful role in serving a purpose that touches your heart. Many computer games attempt to simulate this by offering players central roles in epic adventures. But you don't need to step into cyberspace in order to experience a gripping plot; there are many unfolding around us now. I'd like to take the story of Peak Oil as an example.

Once an oil field is past the peak of production and into the second half of its life, extraction from it becomes more costly and difficult. The same is true of the world's supplies as a whole; as a result, when more than half the global reserves have been used up, oil will become progressively more expensive. This is referred to as Peak Oil. Increasing numbers of experts within the oil industry believe we are beginning to reach the period of Peak Oil now. Dr Colin Campbell,[12] a respected petroleum geologist who's worked in the oil industry for decades, puts it like this:

The first half of the oil age now closes. It lasted 150 years and saw the rapid expansion of industry, transport, trade, agriculture and financial capital, allowing the population to expand six-fold. The second half now dawns, and will be marked by the decline of oil and all that depends on it.

It was Thom Hartmann's book *The Last Hours of Ancient Sunlight*[13] that alerted me to the possibility of world oil supplies beginning to run out within my lifetime. I'd never seen any reporting of this issue in newspapers or on television. As a consequence, I'd not even thought about it. But when I started to take in how much intensive agriculture and food distribution depend on oil, I felt shocked. Cities rely on an industrial system of food supply. If this broke down, what would people eat? My belly went tight as I considered how our society might be heading for a collapse.

Although I found Hartmann's book disturbing, I also found in it a call to adventure. He proposed that those of us living today have a critical role to play in human history. We've already used up half the world's oil reserves.

The next half could go within three or four decades. The way we use those remaining supplies will determine whether our civilization continues or collapses.

The western lifestyle is so dependent on oil that the prospect of its running out is terrifying. As supplies declined, the economy would be likely to go first into recession and then eventually collapse. With the breakdown of industrialized food production and distribution systems, countries like Britain could face food shortages and even starvation. Because this scenario is so disturbing, it is difficult to look at. It tends to get dismissed out of hand and not taken seriously. Yet as an addictions specialist, I'm familiar with the way serious threats can be ignored when they're linked to substances we're dependent on. So I decided to check this one out.

If Thom Hartmann is right, we have a crucial window in time to use the remaining oil to fund a transition to sustainable energy sources. Building solar panels and tidal power stations requires advanced technology. If the oil runs out and industry collapses, we won't have this. So what we do now is vital.

Weaning our society off its oil dependence might seem an impossible task. But when you see your life as an adventure story, you don't expect to have the answers when you're just starting out. Merely to recognize the problem is enough. Then begins the journey of searching for effective responses, and this is what makes the story.

I felt myself activated. I had heard a call to adventure. There was something serious going on and I wanted to do something about it. But how did I know this wasn't just one of those scare stories? This is where the next principle is required.

Seek out the truth

When you come across disturbing information, how do you know it's true? Some stories may get played up. Yet the opposite also occurs. Mainstream media covers such a limited range of issues that it tends to ignore future problems if they are more than a decade or two away. An example of this was in 2004, when scientists announced that levels of carbon dioxide in the atmosphere were rising much faster than expected. This made previous estimates of global warming unrealistically optimistic. While this was reported on the front page of two British newspapers,[14] it wasn't even mentioned in most of the other UK press. If a few media sources report an issue but most don't, people's level of concern may depend on what paper they read.

Such inconsistent reporting brings a need to check the accuracy of information, so that you save your feelings of alarm for where they are really needed. While Thom Hartmann's book seemed well researched, what it said was so shocking that I wanted to check it was really true. So I decided to do my own research. The website of the US Government's Energy Information Administration has an 'ask an expert' service. I asked how long we had before we ran out of oil. Here was the reply:

> *According to our report* International Energy Annual, *world estimated oil reserves are between 1018.7 and 1032.0 billion barrels. In 2001, world oil production was 24.84 billion barrels. If you do the math you will see that world oil resources amount to about 41 to 42 years at current production levels.*

World population is rising, as is the appetite for oil, particularly as countries like China and India become more industrialized. Increasing consumption means that the reserves will be used up more quickly. Feeling concerned, I wrote to my MP, who sent me the UK government's White Paper on Energy.[15] Although this described itself as offering a 'strategy for the long term', I only found one paragraph that took account of world oil supplies as a whole. Here is what it had to say:

> Globally, conventional oil reserves are sufficient to meet projected demand for around 30 years, although new discoveries will be needed to renew reserves. Together with non-conventional reserves such as oil shales and improvements in technology, there is the potential for oil reserves to last twice as long.

The same paragraph went on to say:

> That there is no shortage of oil and gas resources globally means that supplies are unlikely to be disrupted for long.

I puzzled at how the same paragraph could acknowledge that we only had 30–60 years of oil left, but also conclude 'there is no shortage'. Then I looked at the time frame: long term looked as far ahead as the year 2020, while very long term considered up to 2050. From the perspective of separate squares, this may seem as far as is worth looking. If you're over 40, as most policymakers are, you'd almost certainly be dead by 2050. But what about the children of today and their children?

I wrote back to my MP, who passed my letter to Stephen Timms, the Minister for Energy, E-Commerce and Postal Services. In his reassuringly toned reply, he quoted the US Geological Survey, which suggested that there may be large amounts of oil waiting to be discovered. I checked on this and found that the US Geological Survey estimates have little credibility among experts within the oil industry. They refer to probabilities of what might be detected, based on past rates of discovery. Colin Campbell[16] states:

> All the major discoveries were in the 1960s, since when they have been declining gradually over time, give or take the occasional spike and trough. The whole world has now been seismically searched and picked over. Geological knowledge has improved enormously in the past 30 years and it is almost inconceivable now that major fields remain to be found.

How long would you like human civilization to continue for? 50 years? 400 years? 100,000 years? Choices made in our lifetime will have a decisive impact on what that figures turns out to be. If you're on a car journey and have 50 miles' worth of fuel in your tank, that's no problem if you're only travelling a short distance. But if you want to keep going past 50 miles and the petrol pumps are running dry, you need to use less fuel and find new sources of energy. That's the position we're in.[17]

Nuclear power stations have an effective life of a few decades before they need to be decommissioned. The costs of this are huge. Then you have the waste, which remains toxic for hundreds of thousands of years. So the nuclear power option gives moderate short-term benefit for huge long-term cost.

Coal and gas will last a bit longer than oil, but relying on them will destabilize the climate. Greenland has already started to melt; its ice caps consist of enough water to raise sea levels by 7 metres.[18] That would put much of London, New York, Miami, Bombay, Calcutta, Sydney, Shanghai, Lagos and Tokyo under water. While that might not occur for hundreds of years, is this the legacy we want to leave?

What happens in the next three decades will shape the future of humanity for thousands of years. This is the time to decide what to do with the remaining oil. We could fritter it away on things we don't really need. Or we could invest for the future by using it to fund the development of renewable sources of energy.

I realize that what I've presented here is alarming. It can be hard to look at. But there's a problem that may be even bigger than Peak Oil. It is this: when information is too disturbing there is a risk that it gets blanked out. If we don't look at an issue, we can't find our power to respond to it. From my work in the addictions field I've learnt that there is a way to protect ourselves from the danger of denial. The next principle describes what this is.

Allow yourself to feel disturbed

If, in seeking out the truth, you come across disturbing information, there is a reaction that is completely appropriate: feeling disturbed. Remaining completely unbothered may suggest that the information hasn't sunk in deep enough to activate an effective response.

When I'm counselling people with addiction problems, part of my role is to help them recognize areas where their behaviour is out of step with their core values. In motivational interviewing,[19] the term for this is 'developing discrepancy'. When you identify things you're doing that you don't feel good about, it feels uncomfort-

able. But it is the discomfort of this discrepancy that motivates change.

If a parent's heavy drinking is causing problems in their
children, this clashes with the part of them that values
being a good parent. There are two main ways to reduce
discrepancy. One is to alter the information, the other is
to alter the behaviour. A heavy-drinking parent can alter
the information by minimizing it, looking the other way
or through denial. But if they feel supported to take an
honest look at what's going on and they allow themselves
to feel disturbed, then they are more likely to want to
change their drinking.

To tackle a problem you need to notice it; uncomfortable feelings are good at grabbing attention. But the crucial change point lies in the *response* to these feelings.
Some people can't tolerate being upset, so they rely on
addictive behaviour to blot it out. That's part of what
keeps them hooked. The clients I see recover are the ones
who've been shaken *and* stirred. They're shaken up when
they see where they're heading and this shocks them. If
they listen to the shock rather than blot it out, this stirs up
the will to change. This becomes their call to adventure.

There is a strong parallel here to facing global issues.
If you feel upset or concerned about disturbing events in
our world, this can be good news. It shows you've noticed
that something is amiss. It is disturbing to feel the discrepancy between how things are and how they need to be
if life is to thrive in the future. Feelings of disturbance can
act as the inspirational dissatisfaction that calls you into
the adventure of positive change. Worry about the world
can be what launches the process of finding a constructive
response.

> **Try this: A call to adventure**
> *Try these open-ended sentences either in writing, or with a friend:*
> ◆ *When I consider the condition of our world, I think things are getting...*
> ◆ *The feelings I have about this include...*
> ◆ *What I do with these feelings is to...*

It is our emotions that call us. When we're unmoved, we tend to remain stationary. So it is useful to notice what you do with your feelings. Does the call get shut out? Or does it rouse you?

There's still a problem if you feel concerned about an issue but believe it is beyond your power to do anything about it. This is where you need a different way of thinking about power. The next principle provides this.

Understand about level shift

Each time separate parts act together as a whole, the shift in level from parts to whole can lead to new capabilities. This means that you can't predict what's possible just by looking at individual parts themselves. Here's an example.

Termite colonies build nests over 9 foot tall that can live for 100 years. The temperature and humidity in these nests remain remarkably constant, as groups of termites open or close air passages, depending on whether the nest needs warming or cooling. When you look at a single termite, it is difficult to believe that it could play a role in such an advanced system of air conditioning. But level shift is where the shift in level from parts to whole makes new things possible. In this case, temperature control of the nest is an emergent property. It develops when termites act together as a colony (see Figure 11.2).

Figure 11.2 It is difficult to see our potential if we only consider individual abilities

If we only consider our individual actions, it might seem impossible that we could make any difference to global issues. But when we understand about level shift we recognize our part in something larger, the combined effect being more than the sum of its parts. This collective power can work either positively or negatively. Management consultant and author Peter Senge[20] acknowledges this when he says:

> There's not a single individual on the planet who could eliminate a species, if he or she tried. And yet, collectively, we do a splendid job of that without even making the slightest effort.

A single termite is easily dismissed as insignificant. But termites have an appetite for wood and a termite colony can, by eating away at weight-bearing timber, make a house unsafe to live in. Humans have an appetite for wood as well; much of the world's forest cover has already gone. When we destroy so much of nature, we eat away at the planetary equivalent of weight-bearing timber. We're only just beginning to understand how forests act as part of a larger whole in regulating climate and maintaining ecological balance. While termites can trash one house and move on to the next, our planet is the only home we've got. We depend on it.

When you look at a termite and ask 'What's it part of?' you see how it contributes to something larger than itself. We can apply the same approach when viewing our actions and choices. The packaging in supermarkets may once have been part of a tree or, if plastic, part of our planet's oil reserves. It can also be seen as part of a throw-away culture that turns forests and oil into rubbish. In turning away from unnecessary consumption or waste production, a larger change can happen through us. This is *power through*. We might not see its potential when we look at each small step in isolation. To recognize this power, we need a level shift in how we look. Then we appreciate how all our choices count.

If you look at a newsprint photo through a magnifying glass, all you see are tiny dots. But if you step back and look at the picture as a whole, a level shift occurs and the image emerges. When we are just a small part of something larger, we are like one of those newsprint dots. It can be difficult to appreciate that something vaster is going on. When we do get a sense of that bigger picture and feel ourselves as part of it, a deepening of personal power can occur. Applying the next principle makes it easier to experience this.

Use personal power tools

A hurdle that often blocks people is disbelief, particularly if they think: 'You can't change the world, so there's no point even trying.' A useful question with limiting beliefs is: 'What is the effect of thinking this way?' Would women have got the vote if the suffragettes thought like this?

The way through limiting beliefs is to apply the personal power tools introduced in this book. Challenging the thoughts that block you is one way forward (see p 117). Another tool is imaginary hindsight (see p 69). First you identify what you'd like to happen and then you imagine yourself in that desired future. From this visionary perspective, you look back in time and tell the story of how your desired change occurred. You can do this for giving up smoking, losing weight or making business decisions. You can also use it as a way of identifying steps towards a better world.

Try this: Telling the story of the Great Turning

Using the power of your imagination, time travel in your mind to a make-believe future 400 years from now. In this version of events, humanity has found a way through the difficult challenges it faced. The climate has stabilized, people no longer starve and we have developed a flourishing society that lives in balance with our world. Look around you, see what this looks like, imagine that you are really there.

A small crowd gathers around you, as you are the storyteller-historian. They are interested in what you have to say. 'Tell me about the Great Turning,' one of them asks. 'Tell me how they turned things around.' You know the historical period they are referring to: the early twenty-first century. The first 30 years of this formed a crucial turning point in human history. Those were the last decades of the oil age. It was the time when the energy of wind, wave and sun began to be harvested on a mass scale. Tell the crowd how the Great Turning happened. Let your account begin at the time when it may have seemed impossible.

It was Joanna Macy[21] who first told me the story of the Great Turning. As I sat and heard her speak, I felt a tingle down my spine. The changes required in our time are comparable in scale to the agricultural and industrial revolutions. If we are to make a Great Turning to life after the oil age, we need to change our whole way of living. To succeed in this, we need to train ourselves to find our power. The next principle can help you take your experience of this a level deeper.

Let your deeper purpose act through you

When I play music with others, there are times that the group gels and music seems to just flow out of us. On one level we're separate individuals, but on another it's as though the group functions as a larger whole that plays through us, its parts. When these times happen, my playing can be taken to new heights. Afterwards I feel amazed and wonder how it happened.

I've spoken to many people who've experienced something similar to my musical flow through, but in activities quite unrelated to music. They described being in the right place at the right time and stepping forward to play their part in a larger process. When they did this, they said it didn't feel like just them doing it. It felt like something bigger was acting through them. One friend had this while giving a public talk, another while setting up a mental health project. They both felt strangely carried by events, as though there were an unseen force helping them.

Ideas like being 'acted through' may not make much sense if we only think of ourselves as separate individuals. But these experiences are completely understandable from the perspective of a scientific approach called systems thinking.[22] The systems approach has been around for over 50 years and is widely used in medicine, ecology, business consultancy, computer science and family therapy. Systems thinking focuses on how individual elements act together as larger wholes, or systems; it looks beyond isolated events to see the patterns that connect them. With this way of thinking, a system can be seen to act through its parts. Examples include a termite colony regulating its temperature through the combined action of individual termites, or a well-functioning team acting through its members.

Something found in strong teams, but that isn't there when people work alone, is team spirit. This is the feeling of connectedness that leads team members to care about us as well as me. It is the experience of being part of a circle rather than just a separate square. Team spirit is something that acts through people.

When individuals find themselves in a group for the first time, the feeling of team spirit might only be there as a seed, as a potential not yet realized. For it to sprout and grow, there needs to be a shared purpose that people believe is best served by acting together. In a self-help recovery group, that purpose is supporting each other get well; in a work group, the common task is usually related to the job. When a shared purpose acts through people, it creates a bond between them. A buzz can be generated that enhances performance. At a certain point a gelling may occur: no longer merely separate individuals, a sense of us-ness develops. This is level shift.

During periods of crisis there can be an intensification of purpose. When groups rise to the challenge and pull together, team spirit grows stronger. Group identity acts through, and is helped by, individual choices. It is also possible to weaken team spirit. All you have to do is forget that you are part of a team.

When team spirit acts through people, it strengthens their feeling of belonging and inspires them to act for collective wellbeing. Spirituality is like this, but on a much larger scale. It is the feeling of being connected with, and part of, a much larger circle. This feeling of connection can lead to a deepening of personal power in a number of ways.

If you're open to the idea of something larger acting through you, this can change your assessment of what is possible. From this perspective it isn't just you acting; there is also some deeper power giving added support. On one level this is a spiritual understanding of power, but it also makes sense within the scientific framework of systems thinking. Just think in terms of wholes acting through their parts. When you identify with a larger circle, whether that be a team, a community or even life itself, you can think of it as acting through you.

The idea that life may act through us fits with one of the big new ideas of holistic science. Gaia theory views the Earth as a whole, recognizing ways in which it regulates itself to keep in balance.[23] Modern humans seem to have forgotten that we are part of this larger team. We've lost the team spirit. But if we think of ourselves as part of the larger circle of life on Earth, perhaps this bigger team spirit can act through us.

When you serve something larger than yourself, you're never acting alone. You may find yourself with unexpected allies. People you've never met before will help you; a wider network of support and resources becomes available. Joanna Macy[24] uses the term 'grace' for this. Here is how she describes it: 'Grace is the realization that you are part of something larger and receiving from it.'

When you act for a purpose that is shared with others, you also become part of such a network of support for them too. Even if you're doing something tiny, a larger purpose can still act through you. Sometimes you may play a leading role, sometimes a support role. Either way, when a deeper purpose acts through you, so does its power.

> **Try this: Opening to your deeper purpose**
> *If you could act for a deeper purpose in your life, what would it be?*
> ◆ *Identify a step, no matter how small, that moves this purpose forward.*
> ◆ *Take the step. See if you can repeat this process every day.*
> ◆ *Notice how this improves the quality of your life.*

The deepest shifts in personal power occur when we open to something larger acting through us. Like the enhanced playing ability I had when experiencing musical flow through, when deeper purposes act through us this can bring out qualities and abilities we didn't know we had. To experience this power through, we need to think of ourselves as an expression of a circle rather than only a single square. This is stepping into a different story of who we are and what we're capable of. It's an exciting story that can raise the quality of our lives. But to really enjoy doing this is a learnable skill. The next chapter shows how.

266   The Power of Deeper Purpose

Power Points

1 Three routes to increasing life satisfaction are the pleasant life, based on pleasurable activity; the engaged life, based on applying your strengths to absorbing challenges; and the meaningful life, based on serving a purpose that contributes to a bigger picture.

2 Pleasurable activities feel good while they last, but if repeated too often lose their appeal. You get used to them. Serving meaningful and engaging purposes is a more reliable way of gaining long-term fulfilment.

3 Purpose grows out of your way of looking at the world and the myth or story you see your life as expressing. If you only see yourself as a separate individual, purpose may be limited to personal advancement. But identity is also based on what you feel part of. Deeper purposes come from identifying with, and acting for, something larger than yourself.

4 When you feel part of a family or community, it meets personal needs of connectedness and belonging. It also anchors you in a larger story that stretches over longer time periods. In 100 years you, as an individual, will be dead. But the larger you, in terms of the family or community you are part of, will hopefully still be around. This makes the long-term consequences of your decisions more relevant.

5 Many great adventures share the same basic plot: a community faces a threat to its survival and the story is of how the main characters respond. This storyline exists in the larger context of our lives too. Among the threats that human society faces are climate change, increasing toxic contamination of the environment and overdependence on oil, a resource that will begin to run out over the coming decades.

6 The tool of imaginary hindsight can be applied to our world situation. This involves looking back in time from the perspective of an imaginary future that you would like to see occur. Perhaps in hundreds of years, humans will look back on the early twenty-first century as a crucial turning point in history. They may be talking about you and something you were part of.

7 When you act for something larger than yourself, it can act through you. This is where the deeper shifts in personal power can occur.

12

Making It Enjoyable

When I first moved into my home, the garden was completely paved over with concrete slabs. It had at one time been a car park. To turn this dead space into something beautiful and vibrantly alive was a massive undertaking. To achieve this, I organized three 'dig-up-my-garden parties'. I invited friends to bring spades, musical instruments and a willingness to work. They were fantastic occasions that combined fun, socializing and shared labour to bring about a landscape miracle.

Personal power is sometimes associated with images of strict discipline, grim determination and self-denial. There are times when sweat and focus are necessary, but my inner-city garden, now highly productive in fruit, herbs and nuts, reminds me how much can be achieved when we make what we do enjoyable. If the process of improving our lives, work or world gets too grim, we won't last the course. To stick with the journey of change, it needs to be attractive to us. Making what we do enjoyable is therefore deeply pragmatic.

This chapter introduces eight principles that you can apply to any task or activity to bring out more joy in it. These are:

- ◆ *A both/and approach.*
- ◆ *Power with yourself.*
- ◆ *Keeping an eye on the process.*
- ◆ *Having good reasons.*
- ◆ *Experiencing mini-victories every day.*
- ◆ *The right level of company.*
- ◆ *Finding your passion point.*
- ◆ *From maximizing to optimizing.*

A both/and approach

A characteristic feature of satisfying experience is that it engages you. You become absorbed in what you're doing, time passes quickly and you're not wishing you were somewhere else. In 2001, the Gallup organization surveyed American workers to find what proportion felt like this in their jobs.[1] 55 per cent were 'not engaged' and another 19 per cent were 'actively disengaged' – they weren't just unhappy in their jobs, they also regularly voiced their dissatisfactions to colleagues. These figures suggest endemic unhappiness in the workplace.

Part of the problem is the widespread belief that you can't, or shouldn't, mix business with pleasure. Because of this, not much attention is given to designing jobs to be enjoyable. As a result, work is often seen as a negative thing you have to do in order to earn the money you require for the things you like. This either/or split between business and pleasure needs to be questioned.

When large sections of the population are doing jobs they aren't engaged in or don't find satisfying, we need to ask why. What is the purpose of our society? Is it to create an unhappy workforce with money who then buy things to cheer themselves up? Research shows that once basic needs have been met, consumerism isn't an effective long-term strategy for increasing happiness. More materialistic people, at all income levels, tend to be less satisfied with their lives.[2]

Our world also can't afford this approach – if everyone lived a western consumer lifestyle, we would need another four planets to provide the materials and cope with the waste.[3] As it is, the richest 20 per cent of the world's population, most of whom live in western industrialized countries, take over 80 per cent of the global income.[4] If work was more enjoyable, we might not require consumerism to console us; resources could then be shared more fairly. For instance, providing adequate food, clean water, family planning and basic education to the world's poorest people would cost less than is spent each year on ocean cruises, make-up, perfume and ice cream.[5]

Having a disengaged, unhappy workforce is not the most effective way to run a business either. The costs to organizations include increased sick leave, higher staff turnover and lower productivity. Many of our capacities, including our problem-solving ability, improve when we're happier.[6]

Lastly, if we accept it as normal for work to often be a negative experience, we neglect one of the areas with the richest potential for increasing life satisfaction. People in employment spend much of their lives in their jobs. What is needed is a both/and approach that combines business with pleasure and effectiveness with joy.

Although this might initially appear idealistic, I am increasingly being asked by organizations to help them look at how they can achieve this. It is expensive to continually advertise, recruit and train new staff. A cost-effective way of retaining skilled personnel is to redesign their jobs so that they become more satisfying.

The same principle of both/and applies to any task or change you want to maintain. If losing weight, writing a book or activism for the world is seen as a miserable activity, you're less likely to stick at it. Whatever it is you want to do, making it enjoyable helps you to keep doing it for longer.

Power with yourself

Mary always drove herself hard. When faced with a challenge, she would attack it by forcing herself to do whatever was required to get the task done. She did well in college, getting a first-class degree. But she wasn't happy. Working long hours in her job, it was important to her always to succeed. She felt driven by a hard, commanding voice inside. Eventually it drove her to a nervous breakdown.

A common cause of burnout is forcing yourself to continue working when you are beyond your limits, in a way that neglects your needs. After a while, your inner batteries go flat. Mary would often work through lunch breaks, missing meals to get work done. Her approach might initially have appeared productive, but it was based on a slave-driver mentality of having power *over* herself. She forced herself to do things by psychologically whipping herself into action. This squeezed the joy out of her life.

Mary's breakdown marked the beginning of her recovery. The experience of having to stop work led to a major rethink of her life's direction and values. She went through an internal cultural shift, becoming less hard on herself and beginning to take her own needs seriously. She began to hear a softer, kinder voice inside. She was learning to have power *with* herself. *Power with* refers to the strengths that grow out of good relationships. This includes the relationship you have with yourself.

> *Try this: Are you a good employer?*
> *If you were to think of yourself as your own employer, are you a good one?*
> ◆ *Does your workforce (that's you) have regular breaks?*
> ◆ *Do you give yourself encouragement when you're doing things well?*
> ◆ *Could you make the 'job' of your life more satisfying?*

When you apply the approach of power with to yourself, the goal is to develop a sense of teamwork between the different parts within you. This involves developing an inner democracy where you listen to and value the different aspects of yourself. In contrast, the inner slave-driver approach is more like a dictatorship, where dissenting voices are ignored. The problem with this is that rebellious parts of ourselves can express themselves as addictive behaviours, illness or self-sabotage.

Keeping an eye on the process

How would you know whether you had a rebellious aspect that sabotaged you? One way of noticing is to pay attention not just to *what* you are doing (content) but also *how* it is being done (process). Do you have energy for your task? Do you have a sense of willingness? Or is there a resentful sluggishness that grumbles about each step? When a supportive coach notices an athlete going through an off patch, they might ask: 'What's going on?'

We need to do this to ourselves. Noticing and understanding our own resistance is an important step in moving beyond it.

When I give lectures or run groups, I keep track of where people's eyes are. If I see them looking out the window, it suggests I'm losing their interest. By paying attention to the process of engagement as well as my subject, I notice when people are with me and when they're not. Distraction in the audience is a signal that I need to re-engage them. It might be that I've been on a particular topic too long and need to move on (change content); or it might be that I need to approach the same topic in a different way (change process).

The same principle applies with ourselves too. When our eyes are somewhere different to the task in hand, it is a sign we've lost interest. The way to maintain engagement is to notice when we don't have it, and then respond in a way that brings us back in. This might involve having a tea break or a change of subject. It could also involve approaching the same subject but in a different way. By watching our process like this, we get to notice what pulls us in and what switches us off. We can then develop ways of actively re-engaging ourselves when we need to. The more engaged we are, the more we tend to enjoy what we do.

Having good reasons

As a child, I had piano lessons. My great skill was in getting my teacher to talk about her holidays. The more time we spent on that, the less obvious it would be that I hadn't practised much. I had my Grade III exam coming up and I was expected to play for an hour a day; the trouble was,

I didn't enjoy it. I would go through the motions when my parents were around, but because I hadn't yet discovered the joy of music, I couldn't see the point of it. It seemed a boring waste of time.

Intrinsic motivation (see p 20) is where you are drawn to something because of how it makes you feel inside. Imagine if the grading system for musical study was based on this. When you like music you have the first level of musicality. That's the starting point. So all you have to do to get Grade I is find a piece of music you enjoy listening to. You get Grade II if you fancy the idea of playing an instrument. If you want to learn, you look forward to lessons rather than dreading them. Grade III is awarded if you can make sounds on an instrument and gain pleasure from this. It might just be a few notes, but if you enjoy it, you'll want to do it again. The more you do it, the better you get; the better you get, the more you enjoy it. This creates a self-amplifying loop (Figure 12.1).

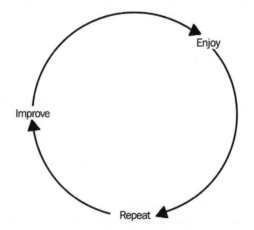

Figure 12.1 A self-amplifying loop of enthusiasm

In her book *The Artist's Way*, Julia Cameron[7] writes:

> *being an artist requires enthusiasm more than discipline... As with all playmates, it is joy, not duty, that makes for a lasting bond.*

Joy gives you a good reason to keep coming back to something. It pulls you in. If you have this at the start of learning an instrument or anything else, it can set off a self-amplifying loop that keeps the process going.

So what about changes that seem necessary but not much fun at all, like giving up smoking or going on a diet? How do we keep ourselves going with these? The joy of successful habit change is based on developing a different kind of delight. Psychologist Martin Seligman makes a distinction between pleasure and gratification.[8] Pleasure is the pleasant feeling you get when you do something you like; gratification is the warm afterglow you get after you've done something you feel good about. Learning the skill of cultivating and strengthening gratification is the key to making difficult tasks enjoyable.

In my addictions recovery work, I use the terms 'one-step' to refer to the immediate consequences of a behaviour and 'two-step' to the delayed effects. The one-step of a drink may be relief or enjoyment, but the two-step is often continued drinking, leading to depression, anxiety and other problems. If the focus is only on the one-step, then giving up is seen as having a pleasure taken away. But when attention shifts to the two-step, reasons for change become clear.

If you have a craving for something you don't really want to do, then you're faced with a challenge. Focusing on the two-step makes it easier to deal with cravings without giving in to them. When you succeed in doing this, you're likely to experience a burst of gratification afterwards.

I see this in the faces of my clients. If someone has had a difficult weekend but not drank alcohol, they have a look of delight on their face. They are with the afterglow of gratification. If they've relapsed, they tend to be more depressed (see Figure 12.2). One ex-client put it like this: 'If I drink I may feel better, but I know I'm getting worse. In recovery sometimes I feel worse, but I know I'm getting better.'

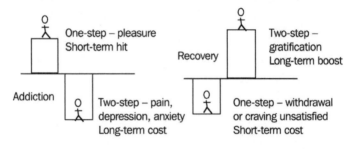

Figure 12.2 The one-step, two-step model

When someone has experienced the afterglow they get from successfully fending off cravings, their recovery is strengthened in a way that gives them a long-term boost. I see people become happier as they feel better about themselves.

There is a similar dynamic at play when facing ecological issues. It might seem that tackling climate change or Peak Oil involves having pleasures taken away from you. But that's only if you focus on the one-step. There may be a short-term cost similar to withdrawal symptoms as the transition is made to a lifestyle and economy that don't wreck the world. The two-step more than compensates for this. There is the deep satisfaction of knowing that you've played a role in making the future more secure for the next generation. When you see good reasons behind what you do, even if it is challenging at the time, the afterglow of gratification becomes a source of joy.

Experiencing mini-victories every day

Something that saps enjoyment is the experience of defeat. While failure may be an inevitable part of life, if you have too much of it, it grinds you down. This is true in games, sports, work, exams, relationships, political campaigns and attempts at weight loss or habit change. When you keep losing, it is not enjoyable and your enthusiasm dies away.

If you are feeling defeated in an area of your life, the following five questions can help you turn things around. By asking these regularly and taking the steps that emerge from them, you can achieve a state where you experience mini-victories every day. This is a way of increasing enjoyment.

> **Try this: Experiencing mini-victories every day**
> ◆ *How do you define success?*
> ◆ *How would you know when you are succeeding?*
> ◆ *What are the steps towards this?*
> ◆ *What achievable step can you take towards this in the next 24 hours?*
> ◆ *What steps have you taken, no matter how small, in the last 24 hours?*

Part of my work is training doctors in how to help people with alcohol problems. This is an area where they commonly feel defeated; as many as 80 per cent believe that there isn't much they can do.[9] Yet their pessimism is often related to how they define success. For every 100 patients a family doctor sees with an alcohol problem, only a small proportion want to stop drinking. Of those who want to stop, only a few will succeed in doing this straight away. So defining success as someone stopping drinking makes disappointment likely.

The way I help doctors turn their pessimism around is by exploring how distant goals always have many steps leading towards them. With behaviour change, these steps are mapped out in the 'stages of change' model developed by psychologists Carlo DiClemente and James Prochaska.[10]

Before we do something differently, we usually make a *decision* to do that. Before making a decision, there is a *contemplation* stage where we think about the issues. If we trace back further in time, there was a *pre-contemplation* stage when change hadn't even crossed our mind. Once we've decided that we want to make a change, the *preparation* stage involves looking for ways to do this. When we know what to do, the *action* stage can begin. However, the direction of change can go both ways. At any point there may be second thoughts or a *relapse*. That's why it is necessary to have a *maintenance* stage once the first steps have been taken, so that gains can be built on (see Figure 12.3).

Doctors often experience frustration because they focus on the action stage of changing behaviour, while the patient may not yet have accepted that they have a problem. For example, patients with stomach pain, sleep problems, depression or anxiety may not have realized that these are either caused, or made worse, by heavy drinking. Just raising the issue of alcohol, so that someone begins to

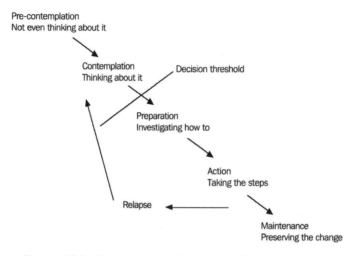

Figure 12.3 The stages of change model

think about it, is a step. If they are already thinking about change, listening to their concerns can be a way of helping them come to a decision. If they want to change, the next step may be exploring what options there are for doing this. By identifying the stage the patient is at and focusing on an achievable step from there, helping people change becomes much more satisfying.

The same principle of translating long-range goals into achievable steps can be applied to any area of change. The scaling questions technique (see p 89) offers a way of doing this. If you identify steps that you can take in the next 24 hours, then you can experience success every day. For a recovering alcoholic, the target of a day at a time means that every 24-hour period without a drink is a victory. It can be broken down even further: when going through a difficult patch, just five minutes without a drink is an achievement. Each mini-victory gives a boost of gratification. This helps build confidence for the next step.

Some issues are so big that it is easy to feel over-whelmed and defeated by them. What's useful about the stages of change model is that it shows how the first steps of change take place inside our mind and heart. Becoming aware of an issue moves us from pre-contemplation to contemplation. Just thinking about something is an active step, as this can bring us closer to a decision. And making a decision to tackle an issue is itself a success, as is any time we recommit to that decision. All of these internal steps precede and prepare us for the more visible steps that others can see.

If you're not sure what to do, finding out more about the issue and possible responses becomes the focus of the preparation stage. Each time you ask a question and take steps to find an answer, that's another mini-victory. Ghandhi once said: '100 per cent effort is 100 per cent success.' Even to have 10 per cent effort may be a success if previously there was less than this. When you want to move towards a goal or have a concern you want to respond to, any step, no matter how small, is a mini-victory.

The right level of company

Joanna Macy has been active in raising awareness about the dangers of radioactive waste for over 30 years. I was interested in how she kept herself going in such a depress-ing area of concern. I was also impressed by her level of knowledge and wondered how she kept herself up to date. She told me her secret. She and her colleagues have developed an approach to making campaigning and activism fun. It is called the study action group.

The starting point is to find others who share a com-mon concern and who are willing to meet regularly to explore ways of responding to it. Joanna felt troubled by the increasing use of depleted uranium munitions and so convened a group to explore this issue. Sessions spent examining the problems of radioactive contamination might not sound very appealing, but these group meetings became the highlight of the week for many who came. How so? The group worked on the following basis:

◆ *Participants took it in turns to research different areas and present their findings to the group. No one had to be an expert. All they needed was a willingness to ask the questions that concerned them and look for answers. Doing this, they learnt from each other.*

◆ *The sessions were divided into three parts: study, strategy and spirituality. That way, factual study was limited to a third of the session. The strategy part looked at how they could respond in terms of campaigning and awareness raising. Through the spirituality component, they developed enjoyable and supportive connections within the group. They'd drum together, have check-ins and have fun.*

◆ *They took it in turns to facilitate the sessions and made a commitment to attend regularly for a fixed period of time. This one was monthly for six months. The group was kept quite small, at fewer than 12 people. That way they built up trust and friendships, as well as all having time to speak in the group.*

For the last year I've been involved in a similar group in Bristol. We meet for a full day every three months, our focus being psychological responses to ecological issues. Looking at concerns like climate change and Peak Oil by myself can be depressing. But when I have the right level of company, it not only strengthens me but becomes enjoyable too.

What I like about the study action group approach is that it can give attention to the process of engagement as well as the content of the subject. If people are getting bored you can shift focus; if they're upset by disturbing information there is space to talk about that. Being based around small groups, meetings can be held in people's homes and they have a much more friendly feel than big public meetings.

You can start a study action group on anything: personal power, environmental concerns, Peak Oil, spirituality, globalization, you choose. Ask yourself: 'What would I like to find out about? What would I like support in facing or dealing with? Who else do I know who shares similar concerns or interests?' Invite them round and start talking about the idea.

Finding your passion point

When you start keeping a watch on your level of engagement, you begin to notice the times when you feel switched off to what you're doing. You may be there physically, but emotionally you're somewhere else. How do you feel about these times? Sometimes it can be a relief to have a simple activity that allows the brain to switch off. But it is also possible to get so stuck in the habit of doing something that you continue it even when you're not enjoying it. Television is a good example.

People in industrialized countries watch television for an average of nearly three hours a day.[11] If you live till you're 75, that's the equivalent of 9 years full time in front of the box. Research has shown that the more people watch, they less they enjoy it. And after watching, they are more likely to feel passive, low in energy and have difficulty concentrating.[12] Too much of this sucks your personal power away. Just imagine what might happen to your life if you had an extra nine years free to follow any interest or purpose?

The danger of being stuck in a rut is that the longer you're there, the less energized you're likely to feel. The one-step is bad, the two-step is worse (Figure 12.4).

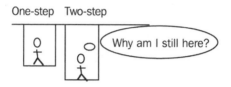

Figure 12.4 Stuck in a rut

By noticing and moving away from situations that drain your energy, you clear the space needed to find and develop your 'passion points'. My friend Dave Bailey uses this term to describe each person's area of maximum enthusiasm. This is more than something you quite like – it is what you love to do or be involved with. When you're at your passion point, you don't need personal power strategies to get started. It may even be difficult to stop.

How do you find your passion points? One clue is to look at your bookshelves. What do you have most books about? Another clue is to notice how you feel when you talk. If certain topics make you come alive, with brightness in your eyes and movement in your body, you've hit the mark.

This is important information. When you spend your life in areas you have your heart in, your vitality increases. And if you're passionate about something, you often

develop skills and knowledge that enable you to contribute in this area. As your experience grows and you're
able to offer more, satisfaction increases over time (see
Figure 12.5).

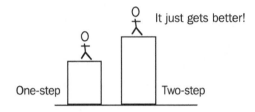

Figure 12.5 At your passion points, satisfaction grows

The Dagara people of West Africa believe that we are
spirit beings who come into human form with a specific
purpose or contribution to make.[13] The mythologist
Joseph Campbell uses the phrase 'finding your bliss' to
describe something similar.[14] Perhaps each of us has several things we are here to do. When you find that sense of
'This is me, this is what I'm here for', it opens up personal
power in a way that is good for you and others too. It's at
your areas of maximum enthusiasm that your purpose can
often act through you most strongly.

From maximizing to optimizing

My friend Dhevdhas Nair is one of the most magnificent
musicians I know. When he plays the piano, I want to stop
whatever I'm doing and listen. His purpose acts through
him in the most beautiful fashion. Yet not long ago he
reached the point where he lost the joy, because he was so
in demand that he played too much. The ancient physi-
cian Galen said: 'The poison is not the substance but the
dose.' Even your bliss can be toxic if the dose is too high.

Personal power is often thought of in terms of maximizing performance and increasing success. But there's a point at which pushing for more of anything becomes at the expense of something else. When you lose the joy, it is a signal. Aiming for too much productivity can lead to overload and burnout. Sometimes more is less. When you move from maximizing to *optimizing*, you let go of the idea that more is always better. There may be a right amount, a right balance. The challenge of finding your power is to discover just that.

Power Points

If the process of improving your life, work or world gets too grim, it won't last. To stick with the journey of change, it needs to be attractive to you. Making what you do enjoyable is therefore deeply pragmatic. Eight principles that help this are:

1 **A both/and approach**: the idea that you shouldn't mix business and pleasure makes for miserable working conditions. Being happier in what you do can improve performance. A both/and approach aims to redesign tasks to make them both productive and enjoyable.

2 **Power with yourself**: power over yourself involves a slave-driver approach that denies basic needs. Power with refers to the strengths that grow out of good relationships. Power with yourself promotes inner democracy. This is like being a good employer of yourself.

3 **Keeping an eye on the process**: by paying attention to the process of engagement as well as the content of what you're doing, you notice when enthusiasm and energy are dropping. You can then take steps to actively re-engage yourself. By doing this you keep your heart in what you do.

4 Having good reasons: it is difficult to be engaged in something if you can't see the point of it. When activities contribute towards purposes that are important to you, they give you an internal boost of gratification.

5 Experiencing mini-victories every day: the way you define success determines how often you experience this. By noticing and valuing the small steps you take in directions that are important to you, you can have mini-victories every day.

6 The right level of company: even the most challenging activities can be made more enjoyable when you have the right people around you.

7 Finding your passion point: when your life is spent in areas you have your heart in, your vitality increases. Passion points are your areas of maximum enthusiasm. This is often where your purpose acts most strongly through you.

8 From maximizing to optimizing: the poison is not the substance but the dose. Pushing for maximum efficiency, income or productivity is often at the expense of something else. 'More is always better' is the slogan of addiction, not recovery.

13

Continuing the Journey

A required piece of reading for scriptwriters in Hollywood is the book *The Writer's Journey* by Christopher Vogler.[1] Having evaluated over 10,000 screenplays for Walt Disney, Warner Bros and other major film companies, Vogler is in a good position to know what makes a plot work. In his book he tells us. He draws on the stages of the hero's journey story structure identified by mythologist Joseph Campbell. These stages don't just make for an exciting movie – they also make for a richly satisfying and exciting life.

The plot begins when a call to adventure inspires the central character of the story to step outside their ordinary life and begin a journey. This call may be based on an attractive opportunity and/or a reason for concern. The deepest calls involve acting for something loved, which is usually threatened by an overwhelming adversary. Rising to the challenge requires courage, skill and the support of allies. Through facing difficulty, a transformation occurs in those taking part in the quest. They emerge stronger, wiser and with greater power. And as a result of their actions, a turning occurs. A situation that initially seemed hopeless changes in unexpected ways.

Vogler refers to the final stage as 'Return with the Elixir'. Here is how he describes it[2]:

> *The hero Returns to the Ordinary World, but the journey is meaningless unless she brings back some Elixir, treasure, or lesson from the Special World. The Elixir is a magic potion with the power to heal. It may be a great treasure like the Grail that magically heals the wounded land, or it simply might be knowledge or experience that could be useful to the community someday.*

In the journey of reading this book, you have come to this final stage.

You have travelled into a world of exploring your dreams and how you move towards them, of finding courage, having breakthroughs, looking and thinking in new ways. You have also encountered disturbing realities, nightmares that could threaten communities you feel part of and, perhaps, also those you love. What is the elixir you bring back? What is the benefit you take from reading this book? And are there any ways you can increase this?

Harvesting the gifts

After attending a course or reading a book, as much as 80 per cent of what you've learnt can be lost in a matter of days. What's good about this is that it stops your head getting filled up with material you might not want to remember. But if you have encountered things you value, there are ways of protecting your memories of these and strengthening the benefits they bring. I think of this as harvesting the gifts. You are now at the harvesting stage and a useful tool for this is the dream cycle.

Review

The first step is simply to review your journey through this book, picking out your favourite bits. When you identify something that's useful to you and give it your attention, you strengthen your memory of it.

> *Try this: Harvesting fives*
>
> *Can you remember five things you valued in this book? If so, write them down. Then see if you can remember another five.*
>
> *How many fives can you harvest?*

Once you've pulled in your harvest, it is worth looking over what you've got. Do any parts stand out? Is there anything here you could see yourself using on a regular basis? Is there anything you're using already? This leads to the next part of the review, which is about acknowledging any recent progress you've made.

> *Try this: Celebrating the steps you feel good about*
>
> *In the time you've been reading this book, are there any steps you've taken that you feel good about? Write them down. Acknowledge your victories, both big and small. When you feel good about what you're doing, you're more likely to keep doing it.*

If you've already taken significant steps forward, just imagine what might happen if you continued this process. And if you haven't moved as far as you'd hoped, what's in the way? Is this something you'd like to tackle? We're moving to the next part of the cycle, which is to look at what you'd like to happen next.

290 Continuing the Journey

Dream

If this book had the best possible effect on you, what might this lead to in your life? A positive vision gives you something to aim for in the planning stage. It also provides motivational fuel to help you move that way.

> **Try this: Imaginary hindsight**
> Imagine that a year from now, you're delighted you read this book. It encouraged you to do something you feel deeply pleased about. What was that?
> Picture yourself there in the possible future you'd like to happen. Now tell yourself the story of the steps you took to get here.

Plan

The first part of planning is developing a clear intention, the second is looking at how you act on that. This stage also gives you an opportunity to look at how you can use the harvest you've pulled in.

> **Try this: Action planning**
> Name three goals you would like to achieve in the next 12 months. For each one:
> ◆ Identify material in this book you can use to help you.
> ◆ Identify an achievable step you can take in the next week.
> ◆ Find a regular time each week to review and repeat this process.

If you'd like to continue the journey of finding your power, it is worth planning how you will do this. Talking with friends about what they've found helpful can open up new leads. I've also listed information about books, courses and resources for developing personal power on my website at www.chrisjohnstone.info.

Moving on

Each time you go round the dream cycle, reach a goal or successfully shift a stuck pattern, you reach an end that also becomes a new beginning. You've reached that point now. It is good to savour the distance you've covered.

But listen... somewhere inside you another journey begins. As Paul Ray and Sherry Ruth Anderson[3] write in their book *The Cultural Creatives*:

> *Our future is not merely something that happens to us, but something that we participate in creating.*

That is our call to adventure.

Notes

Introduction

1 Martin Seligman (1975) *Helplessness*, WH Freeman, San Francisco.

2 Martin Seligman (2003) *Authentic Happiness* (Nicholas Brealey Publishing, London) provides an excellent introduction to the positive psychology approach.

3 J Firth-Cozens (1987) 'Emotional distress in junior house officers', *British Medical Journal*, 295: 533–6.

Chapter 1

1 J Campbell (1993) *The Hero with a Thousand Faces*, Fontana Press, London, p 58.

2 See William Miller & Stephen Rollnick (2002) *Motivational Interviewing* (2nd edn), The Guildford Press, New York.

3 JM Brown & WR Miller (1993) 'Impact of motivational interviewing on participation and outcome in residential alcoholism treatment', *Psychology of Addictive Behaviors*, 7: 211–18.

4 I'm grateful to Colin Campbell, a traditional African healer from Botswana, for teaching me these.

5 Napoleon Hill & W Clement Stone (1990) *Success Through a Positive Mental Attitude*, Thorsons, London, p 26.

6 MORI and Gallup polls quoted in Michael Jacobs (1996) *The Politics of the Real World*, Earthscan, London, p 3.

7 Chris Johnstone (2002) 'Reconnecting with our world', in Anna Chesner & Herb Hahn (eds) *Creative Advances in Groupwork*, Jessica Kingsley, London, Chapter 12.

Chapter 2

1 From *US News and World Report*, quoted in Anthony Robbins (2001) *Unlimited Power* (Pocket Books, London, p 402).
2 Rose Dyson (2000) *Mind Abuse: Media Violence in an Information Age*, Black Rose Books, Montreal, p 77.
3 See James Gleick (1987) *Chaos*, Penguin Books, New York.

Chapter 3

1 JK Rowling (1997) *Harry Potter and the Philosopher's Stone*, Bloomsbury, London.
2 Jim Loehr & Tony Schwartz (2003) *On Form*, Nicholas Brealey Publishing, London, p 94.
3 Mihaly Csikszentmihalyi (1992) *Flow: The Psychology of Happiness*, Rider, London.
4 AM Isen, AS Rosenzweig & MJ Young (1991) 'The influence of positive affect on clinical problem solving', *Medical Decision Making*, 11: 221–27.
5 See Martin Seligman (2003) *Authentic Happiness*, Nicholas Brealey Publishing, London, p 74.
6 See Daniel Goleman (1998) *Working with Emotional Intelligence*, Bloomsbury, London.
7 Paulo Coelho (1995) *The Alchemist*, HarperCollins, London.
8 See J Edward Russo & Paul Schoemaker (1991) *Confident Decision Making*, Piatkus, London, p 111.
9 See Jim Loehr & Tony Schwartz (2003) *On Form*, Nicholas Brealey Publishing, London, p 175.
10 See Joanna Macy & Molly Young Brown, *Coming Back to Life*, New Society, 1998, p 171.

Chapter 4

1 See Martin Seligman (1996) *The Optimistic Child*, Harper Perennial, New York; (1991) *Learned Optimism*, Knopf, New York.

Chapter 5

1 J Campbell (1993) *The Hero with a Thousand Faces*, Fontana Press, London, p 77.

2   JK Rowling (1997) *Harry Potter and the Philosopher's Stone*, Bloomsbury, London.
3   Martin Seligman (2003) *Authentic Happiness*, Nicholas Brealey Publishing, London, p 93.
4   See Anthony Roth & Peter Fonagy (2005) *What Works for Whom?* (2nd edn), The Guildford Press, New York.
5   CB Gesch, SM Hammond, SE Hampson, A Eves & MJ Crowder (2002) 'Influence of supplementary vitamins, minerals and essential fatty acids on the antisocial behaviour of young adult prisoners', *British Journal of Psychiatry*, 181: 22–8.
6   W Gerin, C Pieper, R Levy & TG Pickering (1992) 'Social support in social interaction: a moderator of cardiovascular reactivity', *Psychosomatic Medicine*, 54: 324.
7   Erich Fromm (1957) *The Art of Loving*, Unwin, London, p 15.
8   This is the title of the classic self-help book by Susan Jeffers (1991) Arrow Books, London.

Chapter 6
1   Anthony Robbins (1992) *Awaken the Giant Within*, Simon and Schuster, London, p 258.
2   Edward de Bono (1985) *De Bono's Thinking Course*, Ariel Books, London, p 56.

Chapter 7
1   Gavin Andrews, Richie Poulton & Ingmar Skoog (2005) 'Lifetime risk of depression: Restricted to a minority or waiting for most?' *British Journal of Psychiatry*, 187: 495–6.
2   For a review of these studies and an exploration of the reasons behind this rise, see Oliver James (1998) *Britain on the Couch*, Arrow, London.
3   British Medical Association (1992) *Stress and the Medical Profession*, BMA, London.
4   See Raj Persaud (2005) *The Motivated Mind*, Bantam Press, London, p 56.

Chapter 8

1 Viktor Frankl (1959) *Man's Search for Meaning*, Pocket Books, London.
2 Edward de Bono (1985) *De Bono's Thinking Course*, Ariel Books, London, p 58.
3 HMSO (2000) The BSE Inquiry Report, see www.bse.org.uk.
4 Reported in the *New York Times*, 8 June 2005, viewable at www.commondreams.org/headlines05/0608-05.htm.
5 Susan Jeffers (1991) *Feel the Fear and Do It Anyway*, Arrow, London.
6 Anthony Robbins (1989) *Unlimited Power*, Simon and Schuster, London.
7 TE Oxman, DH Freeman Jr & ED Manheimer (1995) 'Lack of social participation or religious strength and comfort as risk factors for death after cardiac surgery in the elderly', *Psychosomatic Medicine*, 57: 5–15.
8 P Pressman, JS Lyons, DB Larson & JJ Strain (1990) 'Religious belief, depression, and ambulation status in elderly women with broken hips', *American Journal of Psychiatry*, 147: 758–60.

Chapter 9

1 I'm grateful to Prof Patrick Pietroni for introducing me to this metaphor.
2 See Paul Martin (1997) *The Sickening Mind* (Flamingo, London) for an excellent review.
3 JK Kiecolt-Glaser, W Garner, C Speicher, GM Penn, J Holliday & R Glaser (1984) 'Psychosocial modifiers of immunocompetence in medical students', *Psychosomatic Medicine*, 46: 7–14.
4 DT Reilly & MA Taylor (1993) 'The evidence profile', *Developing Integrated Medicine: Complementary Therapies in Medicine*, 1(Suppl 1): 11–12.
5 To find out more about the links between toxic chemicals and rising cancer levels, see UK Working Group on Primary Prevention of Breast Cancer (2005) *Breast Cancer: An Environmental Disease*, www.nomorebreastcancer.org.uk.

6 For more information, see Professor Howard Hu's (2005) lecture 'Environmental Health Hazards', Harvard Medical School, http://chge.med.harvard.edu/education/course/ introduction/hazards/hazards.htm.

7 C Pritchard, D Baldwin & A Mayers (2004) 'Changing patterns of adult (45–74 years) neurological deaths in the major Western world countries 1979–1997', *Public Health*, 118: 268–83. This study suggests dementia has become three times as common in the last 20 years, and environmental toxins may be a causative factor.

8 For a searchable database of these, see http:// database.healthandenvironment.org/.

9 Greg Palast (2003) *The Best Democracy Money Can Buy*, Robinson, London, p 257.

10 To find out about ethical investment, see http://www.ethi-calinvestors.co.uk/why.htm.

Chapter 10

1 Julia Cameron (1995) *The Artist's Way*, Pan, London, p 207.

2 Anthony Robbins (1992) *Awaken the Giant Within*, Simon and Schuster, London, p 78.

3 Charles Horton Cooley (1902) *Human Order and the Social Order*, Scribner's, New York.

4 Howard Gardner (1993) *Multiple Intelligences: The Theory in Practice*, Basic Books, New York, p 9.

Chapter 11

1 Viktor Frankl (1959) *Man's Search for Meaning*, Pocket Books, London.

2 Martin Seligman (2003) *Authentic Happiness*, Nicholas Brealey Publishing, London.

3 In *Authentic Happiness*, Seligman refers to the pleasant life, the good life and the meaningful life. When I attended a course with him in 2005, he used the term engaged life rather than good life. I've used this revision because it is clearer.

4 E Diener (2000) 'Subjective wellbeing', *American Psychologist*, 55: 34–43.

5   Martin Seligman (2003) *Authentic Happiness*, Nicholas Brealey Publishing, London, p 9.
6   See Authentic Happiness newsletter at: http://www.authentichappiness.org/newsletter.aspx?id=54.
7   Mihaly Csikszentmihalyi (1992) *Flow: The Psychology of Happiness*, Rider, London, p 221.
8   David Feinstein & Stanley Krippner (1989) *Personal Mythology*, Unwin, London, p 17.
9   Charles Darwin (1913) *The Descent of Man*, John Murray, London, p 200 (first published 1871).
10 Margaret Thatcher, from interview published in *Woman's Own*, 31 October 1987.
11 Stephen Covey (1989) *The 7 Habits of Highly Effective People*, Simon and Schuster, New York, p 98.
12 Colin Campbell, quoted in article by John Vidal, *Guardian*, 21 April 2005.
13 Thom Hartmann (2001) *The Last Hours of Ancient Sunlight*, Hodder and Stoughton, London.
14 *Independent* and *Guardian*, 11 October 2004.
15 UK Energy White Paper (2003) http://www.dti.gov.uk/energy/whitepaper/ourenergyfuture.pdf.
16 Colin Campbell, quoted in article by John Vidal, *Guardian*, 21 April 2005.
17 The problems start long before oil runs out. After global oil production reaches its peak (the point known as Peak Oil), the available oil gets less each year. This will push oil-dependent economies into decline and eventual collapse. It could also trigger military conflict over remaining supplies. We can reduce these risks by tackling oil dependence before production declines.
18 Hadley Centre (2004) *Uncertainty, Risk and Dangerous Climate Change*, Met Office, UK, p 98.
19 William Miller & Stephen Rollnick (2002) *Motivational Interviewing* (2nd edn), The Guildford Press, New York, p 22.
20 Peter Senge in *What Is Enlightenment?* magazine, Issue 23, 2003, p 47.
21 See www.joannamacy.net. I produce a free quarterly email newsletter about the Great Turning and how to participate in it. To subscribe, see www.GreatTurningTimes.org.

22 For a good introduction, see Joseph O'Connor & Ian McDermott (1997) *The Art of Systems Thinking*, Thorsons, London.

23 For a good introduction, see Jon Turney (2003) *Lovelock and Gaia*, Icon Books, Thriplow.

24 In Christopher Titmuss (1989) *Spirit for Change*, Green Print, London, p 26.

Chapter 12

1 See Jim Loehr & Tony Schwartz, *On Form*, Nicholas Brealey Publishing, London, p 5.

2 See Martin Seligman, *Authentic Happiness*, Nicholas Brealey Publishing, London, p 55.

3 To find out how many planets would be needed for everyone to live at your standard of living, check your ecological footprint at www.myfootprint.org (click low bandwidth if this site fails to load properly).

4 *Human Development Report*, UN Development Program, 1992.

5 *State of the World 2004* (2004) Worldwatch Institute, Earthscan, London, p 10.

6 Alice Isen (2000) 'Positive affect and decision making' in M Lewis and JM Haviland-Jones (eds), *Handbook of Emotions* (2nd edn), The Guildford Press, New York, pp 417–35.

7 Julia Cameron (1995) *The Artist's Way*, Pan, London, p 153.

8 Martin Seligman (2003) *Authentic Happiness*, Nicholas Brealey Publishing, London, p 9.

9 B Thom & C Tellez (1986) 'A difficult business: detecting and managing alcohol problems in general practice', *British Journal of Addiction*, 81: 405–18.

10 J Prochaska & C DiClemente (1984) *The Transtheoretical Approach*, Dow Jones-Irwin, Chicago.

11 R Kubey & M Csikszentmihalyi (2004) 'Television addiction', *Scientific American Mind*, 14(1): 48–55.

12 Ibid.

13 Malidomma Somé (1995) *Of Water and the Spirit*, Arkana Books, New York.

14 Joseph Campbell (2001) *The Power of Myth*, DVD interview with Bill Moyers, Mystic Fire Video, Burlington.

Chapter 13

1   Christopher Vogler (1999) *The Writer's Journey*, Pan, London.
2   Ibid., p 25.
3   Paul Ray & Sherry Ruth Anderson (2000) *The Cultural Creatives*, Harmony Books, New York, p 340.